# The Dylan Thomas Trail

For Rosemary Thorpe

# The Dylan Thomas Trail

David N. Thomas

Photographs by Ken Day

y Lolfa

First impression: 2002
Second Impression: 2003
© David N. Thomas and Y Lolfa Cyf., 2002
Photographs 2001 © Ken Day
Drawing of Majoda © Jacky Piqué
Cover photo of Dylan Thomas: Swansea Archives
Design: Ceri Jones

ISBN: 086243 609 5

Printed on acid free and partly recycled paper
and published and bound in Wales by:
Y Lolfa Cyf., Talybont, Ceredigion SY24 5AP
*e-mail* ylolfa@ylolfa.com
*internet* www.ylolfa.com
*phone* +44 (0)1970 832 304
*fax* 832 782
*isdn* 832 813

# Contents

# Introduction

Dylan Thomas loved walking through the fields and lanes of Cardiganshire – especially if there was a pub at the end with good beer and conversation. He enjoyed the company of local people, and listened with relish to the stories and gossip of the countryside. This guide takes you through some of Dylan's favourite parts of Cardiganshire (today called Ceredigion), including the places that inspired some of his best writing.

The Trail goes through red kite country, beginning in the small seaside town of Llanon, taking you through oak woods and hidden valleys to the Roman road at Tal-sarn. Here the Trail turns back towards the sea, following the kingcupped and kingfishered Aeron valley, where otters hunt sea trout and herons fly overhead like baby pterodactyls. At the Georgian town of Aberaeron, the Trail goes south along the heritage coast of Cardigan Bay. The path takes you through fields of coconut-scented gorse and wind-bent hawthorn, with fine views of the dolphins and seals out at sea, ending up in New Quay, the town that Dylan mostly drew upon for *Under Milk Wood*.

The beautiful countryside of Cardiganshire was in Dylan's blood – his great-uncle, Gwilym Marles, had been a Unitarian minister and radical leader in the county, and a poet of some distinction as well. Dylan had an aunt and cousin living in New Quay, who had moved there in the 1920s, but the family steered clear of him after being warned about his scrounging ways. He had more success with Lord Howard de Walden, who gave him the occasional cheque, and allowed him, during the early 1940s, to work on his poetry at Plas Llanina, de Walden's mansion on the outskirts of New Quay.

From 1941 to 1943, Dylan also stayed in Plas Gelli, a handsome mansion near the river Aeron in Tal-sarn. Dylan's Trail goes through the grounds of the mansion, and it's easy to see why it inspired such marvellous poetry. It was here that Dylan and Caitlin's daughter, Aeron, was conceived, on the banks of the river after which she was named.

Dylan and Caitlin went back to New Quay in 1944 and lived in Majoda, a bungalow on the cliff top overlooking the beach. Dylan's time at Majoda was to be one of the most prolific of his adult life – and one of the most sensational. It was here that a war-weary commando, William Killick, fired into the bungalow with a Sten gun and threatened to blow up Dylan and Caitlin with a hand grenade.

Dylan's Trail goes past Majoda (the bullet holes have long since gone!) and follows one of the routes that Dylan took into New Quay on his daily trips to the pub. It was on these excursions that he would stop and gossip with the townspeople, picking up the material he would use in *Under Milk Wood*. New Quay is still an unspoilt seaside town, a terraced community of colourful houses, shady woods and sandy beaches, with magical views across the sea to Snowdonia. Lobster and crab are landed here, and in summer the fishermen will take you out to see the bottle-nosed dolphins.

The Dylan Thomas Trail also has a lot to offer the amateur historian. It passes prehistoric forts, earth works, Bronze Age burial mounds and the remains of a medieval village. It goes past the eighteenth century walled garden at Tŷ Glyn mansion and the John Nash house at Llanerchaeron, both open to the public. There's also a fascinating array of famous people associated with this part of west Wales: Augustus John, Evelyn Waugh, T.S. Eliot, Compton MacKenzie, Edward Elgar and even King Edward VIII. Not to mention the notorious head of MI5 who travelled from London for gay fishing parties in New Quay...

Ceredigion is a beautiful but demanding land. Its farming economy has often seen difficult times, producing a culture of hard work and thrift. It has been a county of small shopkeepers, with a strong tradition in the woollen and drapery trades. In the 1920s and 1930s, many families moved to London and opened dairies and corner stores. It is also a county that has been dependent on fishing, and the recruitment of its men to the merchant marine. Its people, raised largely in the disciplines of the Nonconformist chapels, have a reputation for learning and self-improvement. The county is host to two university colleges and to the National Library of Wales. There's hardly a page of the *Oxford Companion to the Literature of Wales* that doesn't contain at least one entry for a Cardiganshire man or woman.

I've divided Dylan's Trail into several sections, with a choice of accommodation at the end of each day. It's not an arduous trail and a good deal is along river banks, cliff tops and gentle countryside. But, as always, come well shod, prepared for some rain and with a warm jumper for the coastal section. You could also bring the book *Aberaeron and Mid Ceredigion*, a collection of marvellous period photos that will give you an idea of how the towns and villages you will walk through looked in Dylan's day and earlier. And before you start out, why not read *Quite Early One Morning*, Dylan's own description of a walk around New Quay and universally recognised as the seed bed for *Under Milk Wood*?

I've also written this book for armchair Dylan fans. It contains new information that has emerged since my last book★ on how New Quay's people and places inspired Dylan in the writing of *Under Milk Wood*. I've included the police plan of Majoda drawn after the shooting, as well as the notes of the arresting officer in the case.

There's also new material on how some of Dylan's maternal relatives were connected to New Quay, as well as more details on the way Dylan maintained his New Quay contacts after 1945. Not to mention the first known instance of Dylan's failure to pay a bill, as a sixteen-year-old schoolboy on a walking holiday near Cardigan; and a newly-found, Lampeter-bound letter from June 1953 which contains a chilling premonition of the poet's November death.

★ *Dylan Thomas: A Farm, Two Mansions and a Bungalow*, Seren, 2000, ISBN 1-85411-275-9. The book describes Dylan's Cardiganshire roots and the time he spent there.

# Through Milk Wood: Llanon to Tal-sarn

**8 miles**

## HOW TO GET THERE

**BY BUS:** From Aberaeron or Aberystwyth. There's a railway station at Aberystwyth that connects with mid and north Wales, Birmingham and London.

**BY CAR:** Public parking in front of the White Swan or leave your car in Aberaeron and take a bus or a taxi to Llanon

OS Landranger Maps 145 and 146 Explorer 199

The walk starts at the Central Hotel. In Dylan's day, the landlords were a Mr Mann and a Mr Marks. Dylan probably got on well with them but they were regarded with deep suspicion by the village; not only were they Londoners but they were Jewish, thought to be gay and, worst of all, wore suits that had no pockets.

Dylan came to the Central with his friend Thomas Herbert, the vet. The hotel was Herbert's base camp during his courtship of Tessa Dean, the daughter of Lady Mercy Greville and Basil Dean, the film producer. Tessa lived with her mother in Cwm Peris. The Central was conveniently situated at the start of the long track up the valley to Tessa's house.

Tommy Herbert will crop up several times on this Trail. He did more than anyone else to introduce Dylan to the Cardiganshire countryside. As a vet, he had a war-time petrol allowance, and he would often invite Dylan to come on his daily rounds. He was a sociable man, liked his pint and had a great love of literature, both Welsh and English. He was also one of Dylan's guides to the sex life of New Quay, but more on that later.

Take time in Llanon. There's more to it than meets the eye, so don't dismiss it as just another village on the busy main road to Aberystwyth. Even by the late

1940s, it was one of the wealthiest villages in Wales, "being largely made up of comfortable villas, in which stucco plays no inconsiderable part, and occupied by retired sea captains." Here was an abundance of *capten saith gant* (£700 captains), as historian Ivor Thomas has explained:

> It was the life-long ambition of Llan-non master mariners to build and pay for an impressive home, name it after their most impressive vessel, and retire safely with savings of at least £700.

The wealth shows in the two magnificent chapels and the fascinating church of St. Ffraed's, the patron saint of milkmaids and those working in the dairy trade – there could hardly be a more appropriate patron for our exploration of the *Milk Wood* trail.

The church is down by the sea in the little community of Llansantffraed, which used to be an important ship-building centre. The window in the south wall depicts St. Ffraed with a bowl of milk and a cow behind her. The interior of the church is unusual; it is more like that of a Nonconformist chapel, with a gallery and tall pews with doors.

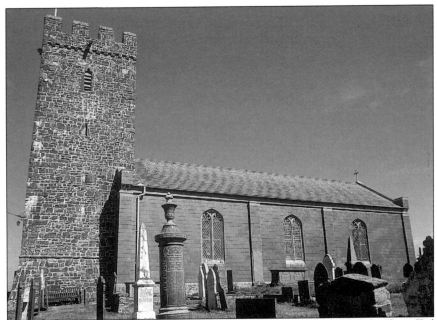

*St. Ffraed's, patron saint of the Dylan Thomas Trail*

There's also another holy presence in Llanon – Dewi Sant (St. David), the patron saint of Wales, whose mother, Non, is said to have been born in the village; some say Dewi Sant himself was born here. Keep Dewi in mind – we shall be close to him for much of the Trail.

Along the coast, half a mile north of St. Ffraed's church, you'll find a fine group of lime kilns. The geological strata on the cliff have been classified as a Site of Special Scientific Interest.

Mediaeval strip fields still survive in the village, and you can walk amongst them on the land between the main road and the sea. Here the plots, or slangs as they are called locally, are still owned by many different people. Just behind the Post Office is one of the last surviving cottages in west Wales with an original straw rope underthatch. It's open in August.

Sightseeing over, head for the Old Mill Bakery on the main road, at the Aberaeron end of the village. This is a good place to buy your lunch, as there are only two pubs on the route between Llanon and Tal-sarn. If you do fancy a pub lunch, then ring ahead to the Ship at Pennant or the Poacher's Pocket in Cilcennin to make sure they'll be open. Likewise, there are only a couple of guest houses at the Tal-sarn end, so you'll need to book your bed in advance.

If you can drag yourself away from the bakery, take the turning opposite to Pennant. Climb the hill to the sharp bend and follow the waymarked path up the stone steps. You will now be entering farmland, so please keep dogs on a lead if there are animals in a field and when going through farmyards. Keep close to the hedge on the right until you find a stile just over half way up the field. Cross over and continue to follow the left-hand hedge to another stile, well defended by stinging nettles, and over into the yard of Pentyparc Farm. Go straight up to the metal gate and across the field (which can sometimes be quite boggy) to the stile you can see in front of you.

Stop here and look behind for a fine view of Cardigan Bay, with, on your right, a sweep of mountains that include Pumlumon, Cader Idris and Snowdonia beyond. On a clear day, you can also see "the northern claw" of the Lleyn Peninsula.

Carry on, following the hedge on your left, to yet another stile. To your right are good views of New Quay on its prominent headland, the "cliff-perched" town as Dylan once called it, where the walk will finish on the third day.

*The path to Milk Wood*

Once over the stile, curve round with the right-hand hedge. Two more stiles bring you to the track down to Penlan Farm. Turn right and walk towards the farm. Follow the waymarkers diagonally across the farmyard towards the metal barn. Go through the gate, heading down the field for the telegraph pole. Descend the steep bank to find the steps, by an oak tree, that will take you across a little stream. Climb up the other side, following the path upwards into a former farmyard. The outbuildings have now been converted into cottages. Walk between them, towards the white house, and up a small flight of steps. You are now outside Wernllaeth Farm.

"Wernllaeth" means "Milk alder grove", but translates more naturally as "Milk Wood" and perhaps it was this farm that helped to inspire the name of Dylan's most famous work. Of course, Dylan didn't know very much Welsh but Tommy Herbert, the vet, was a Welsh speaker, and also took a great interest in the meaning of local place names. We know from his friends that he was always explaining the meaning of Welsh place names to Dylan. The Williams brothers, who lived in Wernllaeth during the war, were regulars in the Central Hotel in Llanon, and it's possible that Dylan might have met them there.

The path continues past the front of the house, along a bramble-lined track, eventually ending at a stile. Follow the left-hand fence along to a waymark post next to a concrete drinking trough, and cross downhill to pass through a metal gate. Veer right, almost diagonally across the field, heading for the fence and trees. Follow this fence around until you come across a stile – it's invisible until you are almost on top of it. Cross the stream, turning left for about twenty metres towards a gate. Don't turn right, but walk straight on, up a lane shaded with oak and alder, with sea views behind. Go right at the junction with the larger road and head downhill into Pennant.

After passing the village school, you'll come to a crossroads. On your left is a small white cottage that dates from the early nineteenth century. It has a thatched roof, covered in corrugated iron, and is a good example of a vernacular cottage now rare in this part of west Wales. Carry on down the hill to find another cluster of interesting architecture. First, the charming bridge over the river Arth. On one bank is Capel Pennant, a Calvinistic Methodist chapel built in 1832, with particularly attractive windows, especially round the back. On the other, the Ship Inn, a lovely little pub that dates back to the 1750s. It was once the haunt of smugglers, who brought their barrels of brandy up the Arth from the coast. Dylan sometimes came here with Tommy Herbert.

Cross the bridge and go through the gate on your left, immediately after the pub car park. The entrance can be wet but the path soon dries out. Follow the hedge round above the river Arth. After about 400 metres, cut across the field in the direction of the farm buildings. This is Wernddu Farm, the darker sister of milky Wernllaeth, for it means "black alder grove". Head to a point about 100 metres in front of Wernddu. Go through the metal gate and turn right to walk up the track to the junction with a minor road, where you go left.

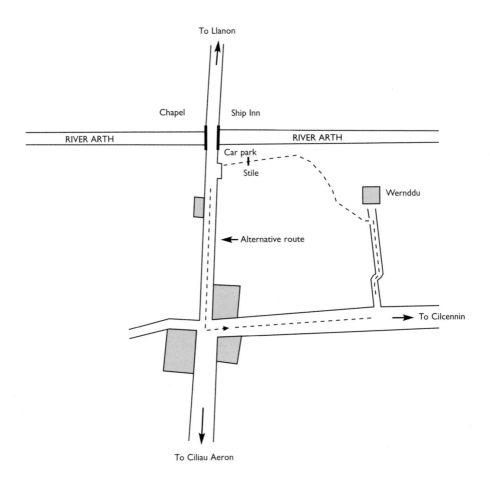

The route will now take you to Tal-sarn by quiet country lanes where the most you will meet are solitary sheep and the occasional tractor. There are fine views from this road, until it descends gently through woodland for about a mile to a T-junction. Turn right and immediately left towards Cilcennin. Keep on this lane until you come to a staggered crossroads, with a white house on one corner and a workshop on the other. This is the studio of artist Gordon Miles – if you'd like to look at his work, call in.

Carry straight on to the centre of Cilcennin, with the Poacher's Pocket pub and its tail of Georgian cottages on one side, and Holy Trinity church on the other. The small stone building across the road from the pub is the *Sgoldy Fach* – the little school house. It was replaced in 1877 by the present school, down the road to your right, next to another fine chapel.

If you were to walk the other way for a mile or so, you'd come to a farm called Llaethdy. This was the birthplace of poet-preacher David Lewis (1870 – 1948), whose bardic name was Ap Ceredigion. He was also a hymn writer, with thirty-three compositions in the Welsh hymn book.

The road to Tal-sarn lies in front of you, about three miles of exhilarating walking along a lane that skirts the ridge above the Aeron valley. After three-quarters of a mile, the road climbs steeply – look back at the sea, because you won't see it again for a while. At the top of the hill, two metal gates face each other across the road. On your right is Castell-y-Bwlch, an Iron Age fort, and on your left a hill called Trichrug, now partly crew-cutted in conifers. This is thought to have been the site of an ancient battle. There are also Bronze Age burial mounds on the summit. Local legend has it that a powerful giant lived on Trichrug who was, said one early guide book, "endowed with the genius of the Aeron Vale." Neighbouring giants were challenged to trials of strength on the summit and on one occasion the Trichrug giant threw a quoit that landed on the shores of Ireland.

There's a footpath to the top of Trichrug and it's worth the climb just for the views. On a clear day, you can see the Brecon Beacons to the east, Pembrokeshire to the south and (almost) Ireland to the west. From the top, there are more wonderful views northwards to Snowdonia and Cader Idris – though you can also see some of the industrial-scale wind 'farms' that are gradually disfiguring the Welsh landscape. Just like the old days, when valleys and villages

*Above Tal-sarn, "in the cloaked hedge row"*

were drowned for clean water and electricity. At least then, tens of thousands in the cities benefited but today the wind factories produce little energy gain and very limited local employment.

Indeed, walkers and their walking provide far more economic benefits to the Welsh economy. So let's turn our backpacks on the wind machines and walk back down the hill to the road, bearing profit and prophecy in equal measure.

Carry on towards Tal-sarn. The next farm on your left is Gwrthwynt, where James Hughes, the dockworker-poet, was brought up, though his birthplace was in Ciliau Aeron, which you'll come to on the second leg of the Trail. Hughes, whose bardic name was Iago Trichrug, went to London when he was eighteen and worked as a blacksmith in the shipyards. He was ordained in 1816 and was the minister at Jewin Chapel, near the Barbican, between 1823 and his death in 1844. He is remembered for his poems, hymns and six volumes of commentary on the Bible. A statue was erected in his memory in City Road, London, opposite John Wesley's Chapel.

The road now opens up with magnificent views on your right of the Aeron valley and, in the far distance ahead of you, the Cambrian Mountains. You'll now find yourself walking above the red kites that hunt through the valley below. This top road was one of the haunts of Dafydd Gwallt Hir, the Aeron's most well-known and colourful tramp. See if you can spot stones near the entrances to farms where the tramps used their knives to carve coded messages to each other about the reception they were likely to get. There were signs for "dogs", "food only", "food and bed", "no money" and "just water".

When you reach the entrance to Caebanadl, look back down the road to see the distinctive outlines of Castell-y-Bwlch. After passing Lluest farm, there's a road on the left that, had you the time, would take you the half-mile or so to Capel Hermon, a small and remote chapel associated with the renowned Welsh preacher, J.D. Jones. Carry on past the turning to Hermon. The road now begins to descend steeply towards Tal-sarn, winding down through a colony of modern houses. About 200 metres after the last bungalow, you'll find a footpath sign on your right, as the road flattens out. Follow this farm track into Plas Gelli.

# A Gent at Gelli

Dylan stayed in Gelli between 1941 and 1943, travelling back and forth between Wales and London, where he was working on wartime film documentaries. He came here at the invitation of his friends, Vera and William Killick. Dylan had been at infants' school with Vera in Swansea and was best man when she married William. Dylan was supported by Vera and William throughout the war, both with money and accommodation at Gelli. Vera's mother, Margaret Phillips, had been born just outside New Quay and she rented Gelli from the beginning of the war. Vera and her mother were an important part of Dylan's Cardi roots.

Gelli was also Dylan's refuge from the war, particularly from the bombing of Swansea. The mansion was his "greenwood keep", as he calls it in his poem *In Country Sleep*. Today, the house seems engulfed by beeches and redwoods, but there were even more trees in Dylan's time.

A number of poems were influenced by Gelli, but there are three of particular importance. *Love in the Asylum* is partly about the ghost that haunts the house, partly about the madness of war. *A Winter's Tale* is set in the flood plain of the Aeron valley. There are many references throughout the poem to Gelli and the surrounding countryside. *In Country Sleep* was written in Italy in 1947; it is dedicated to Dylan's daughter, Aeron, and evokes the lush Welsh countryside that he missed in the oppressive heat and dryness of Tuscany. It's a poem that catches the powerful spiritual atmosphere of Gelli, which was built on the site of an abbey.

The footpath takes you past the farm buildings, hugging the stream on your left. It passes the giant redwood under which Dylan would sit to write. This redwood was once circled by eight beeches, forming a huge, wood-framed, leaf-skinned, sky-touching wigwam in which Dylan sat. It was here, on his stool, under the wood, that Dylan enjoyed his mugs of milk from Princess the cow, brought to him by Mary Davies and her grand-daughter Amanda. This was Dylan's own milk wood.

*Mary Davies and Amanda, aged three, 1937*

Please take care to stay on the path and respect the privacy of those who now live in the house. Keep close to the stream, through the rhododendrons, heading for an old metal gate. Go through the field to the new wooden bridge, which you cross. Turn right and walk across the field, with fine views of Gelli and its trees. Exit along a small lane, turn left and then right. Just before a house called Millponds, turn left through a metal gate into a field. Follow the right-hand hedge all the way down. Cross through a gate into a smaller field and then through four more metal gates next to sheep folds. You'll come out into Tŷ Mawr yard, where some of the buildings have been converted into craft shops. You are now in Tal-sarn.

Tal-sarn is an ancient settlement. Translated, it means 'end of the road', a reference to the Roman road known as Sarn Helen which runs near the village. The village was a centre for a thriving group of poets in the nineteenth century who lived in and around the Aeron Valley. They wrote about the people, places and events of the countryside. The most distinguished was John Jenkins (Cerngoch). John's brother, Joseph (1818–1898), was also a poet, a farming innovator who wrote for the agricultural journals, a pioneer of elementary education in the area, and founder of the Tregaron Cultural Society, which met once a week to discuss literature and current affairs. He went to Australia in 1869 and his diaries have been published as *Diary of a Welsh Swagman*.

Dan Jenkins, Pentrefelin

One of the youngest of these Aeron poets was Dan Jenkins (1856–1946), who came from Pentrefelin Farm, just outside Tal-sarn. He retired there after ending his career as a school teacher, having published a collection of his own poetry. Caitlin used to come to Pentrefelin to borrow ponies for riding across the countryside and in the Tal-sarn races. We also know from Tommy Herbert's papers that Dylan knew Jac, Dan Jenkins' son, who was running the farm. It seems more than likely that Dylan would have passed the time of day with old Dan Jenkins, and might have learnt from him, and from Tommy Herbert, of the talents of the Aeron poets.

You'll have noticed by now that most of the country poets were men. But here, just a mile or so outside Tal-sarn, lived a remarkable local poet called Dinah Davies (1851–1931), who published a collection in 1912. She lived in Tynrhos (SN 565 592) and there's a footpath that takes you past this remote, and now derelict, farm. In fact, this is such beautiful, and gentle, walking country that you should consider spending an extra day or two around Tal-sarn, using the Explorer 199 map to find the footpaths and country lanes. Dinah's grave is in the parish church at Nantcwnlle; you'll find her slate tombstone some twelve metres uphill to the right of the bell tower window.

*Dinah Davies*

Dinah often wrote about the evils of drink, so she would never have gone to the Red Lion in Tal-sarn, but it was Dylan's local when he stayed at Gelli. Today, of course, it's quite unlike the pub that Dylan knew and it's now called the Llew Coch. In Dylan's day, the pub brewed its own beer and had a Public Bar and a Lounge. It was another place where Dylan got to know the locals, and they saw him as a gentleman, a "big bug" from Swansea, as local man Emrys Davies told me:

> Miss Evans thought he was a real gent, a gentleman to be looked up to. He was very well dressed, you know. Every afternoon, Miss Evans called him from the bar 'You ready, sir?' She used to bring the tray with the tea into the parlour, just for him, and he used to accept it, cakes, and best china, lovely jugs, and he was only on his own. He used to drink his tea in there and he used to come back and have some more beer.

If you're staying the night in Abermeurig, you now need to walk along the B4342, signposted to Llangeitho. You'll be in good company, for this was a walk that Dylan greatly enjoyed, as Tommy Herbert has described. You'll pass the hamlet of Llunden Fach, where the poet William Lloyd (d.1911) lived in a pub, the Blue Bell. After three-quarters of a mile, turn right for Abermeurig. The first farm you pass on your left is the Jenkins' Pentrefelin, where Caitlin borrowed the ponies. Next comes a bridge across the Aeron. If you stand here and look across the fields, you'll see Abermeurig mansion, surrounded by huge beech and oak trees. The entrance to the mansion is just a few yards along the road.

But if you're staying in Brynog, you'll need to walk out of Tal-sarn, as described in the next section of the Trail. Abermeurig provides evening meals (by prior arrangement), Brynog does not. But you can eat in the Vale of Aeron pub, only fifteen minutes walk from Brynog. Dylan and Caitlin came here often, and today it still has a special charm and atmosphere. In the church opposite, you'll find the grave of John Davies, another Aeron poet – see page 91 for details of the pub and the poet.

# The Heron Valley: Tal-sarn to Aberaeron

9 miles

OS Landranger Map 146 Explorer 198 and 199

There are no pubs and cafes on this part of the Trail until you reach Aberaeron, though the Tyglyn Aeron Hotel is more than happy to rustle up a pint or a coffee. There are no shops in Tal-sarn to buy the ingredients for a picnic. So better ask your guest house to prepare a packed lunch.

Leave the village past the tractor showrooms. Cross the Aeron by the bridge that Dylan immortalised in his August 1942 letter-poem to Tommy Earp:

> As I tossed off this morning over Talsarn Bridge to the fishes
> At war myself with the Celtic gnats under a spitfire sun...

This is not meant, of course, to be taken literally but as a metaphor for the happiness Dylan felt at Gelli. Once over the bridge, turn right immediately down a track which soon brings you to a footpath that clings to the river most of the way to the sea at Aberaeron. You are now in mansion country: in the six fertile, frequently-flooded miles between Tal-sarn and the coast there are no fewer than eight country houses, nine if you include Nashly Monachty, that looks down on the Aeron from afar. In recent years, the fortunes of these grand houses have been mixed. Some are still in private hands, but of the others, one is a hotel, another the offices of a cheese factory and the last on the river is owned by the National Trust.

For much of this section, you'll be walking across the fields of Llanllŷr Mansion, through which Dylan and Caitlin walked on their way to the Vale of Aeron pub in Ystrad Aeron (Felin-fach). The mansion, built on the site of a twelfth century nunnery, inspired the novel *Lleian Llanllŷr* by Rhiannon Davies Jones. When the path escapes from between fence and river and enters a field, you are in Dolau Dŵr (water meadows). Look to your left to see the mysterious, some say magical, circle of hawthorns, set around a stone wall, now mostly collapsed.

The Aeron cuts deep through the fields here and its banks are teeming with wildlife. It is a river of plenty; not only does it have salmon and sea trout (known locally as sewin), but the very word *aeron* means fruits, berries and grain. It is the river of the autumn harvest. The valley of the Aeron was one of Dylan's favourite places. He relished its peacefulness, as he described in his radio broadcast *Living in Wales*. Dylan spoke of the Aeron valley, Tommy Herbert once said, as "the most precious place in the world."

Half an hour's walking will bring you close to Brynog, on the other bank of the river, another mansion with parkland and fine trees. Two Wellingtonia dominate the field in front of the house. Were these the trees between which the giant of Trichrug hung his clothes line? You leave the path and exit onto a metalled lane. Turn right to cross the river, then bear right for your lodgings or left if you are continuing on the Trail.

You'll come to a crossroads in the farmyard. Turn left towards Berllan-deg Farm. The factories you can see on the far side of the river hardly enhance the beauty of the valley, but they provide much-needed local employment. They process milk from the surrounding farms to make food flavourings and cheeses.

The Aeron is now on your left side, but it can hardly be seen as it wanders through the lush fields towards the sea. Cross Berllan-deg farmyard, exiting through a metal gate that takes you onto a grassy track, which can be wet and muddy in parts. Follow this for about three-quarters of a mile through woodland to a stile. This spot is especially worth visiting in the Spring when the woods are thickly carpeted with bluebells.

You are now on an old, perhaps ancient, track. It was probably part of a route taken by monks travelling to the coast to collect fish from the traps at Aberarth, where, at low tide, you can still see the remains of circular walls of stone. These date back to the sixth century and were used for stranding fish as the tide went out. These traps – *goredi* – were a source of salmon for the mansions of the Aeron valley as late as the 1870s. (You can continue the monkish theme later by travelling to the remains of the Cistercian abbey at Ystrad Fflur – Strata Florida. It's the burial place of Dafydd ap Gwilym, one of Europe's foremost medieval poets.)

Carry on to another stile; the footpath now goes straight ahead. After about fifty metres, turn off left by the waymark post and carry on until you join a forestry track, where you turn left. You'll come to a cottage with barking dogs, taking you up to a country road. Cross over and follow the track on the other side.

## Lenin and Eliot: Resting in Ciliau Aeron

This is the start of the Beech Walk, where T.S. Eliot liked to stroll when he came to the village of Ciliau Aeron to get away from the literary rat-race in London. You'll soon come to a line of giant beeches, interspersed with the stumps of those that came down in recent gales. As you look across, you'll see a large white mansion that today is the Tyglyn Aeron Hotel. In the 1930s, this was the country estate of the publisher Geoffrey Faber, where Eliot used to stay for ten days or so during the summer months.

The path takes you through the old farm buildings of the estate, which have now been converted into homes. Turn left at the road and walk down past the hotel. The house was built for Thomas Winwood, an ironmaster's son from Bristol. Only the left side of the building survives from that period. The remainder was destroyed by fire in 1985 and was rebuilt in the mid-1990s. If you stop for a coffee in the hotel, you'll find a photograph in the public bar of Eliot asleep in Faber's drawing room. Little survives now of the interior that Eliot knew, but we can get a feel of the place from its description when the house was put up for auction in 1955, just fourteen years after Faber had sold it.

Leave the Tyglyn Aeron Hotel and walk down the road to the junction. Pause here and look left. Out of sight, on the other side of the village, are the former Ciliau Aeron railway station, as well as James Hughes' birthplace and two special places of worship. You probably won't have time to walk there but you might want to come back later in a car. For now let's go on foot in our mind's eye, a virtual walk, where the legs never ache and blisters are water cushions:

*Turn left and go down past the old drive to Faber's house with the old gates spared from the war effort, across the old bridge which is two bridges joined together (the very old bridge and the quite old bridge), up the tree-lined road, past the old mill on your left and then past the farmhouse on your right where once lived old David Jones, the* bee's knees on anything to do with apiculture, and then up the little rise to the not-so-old bungalows on the not-so-old estate. Here, at the first bungalow on your left, once stood the old railway station, with its pagoda waiting-room and stylish lamps, where Eliot alighted for the start of his summer holidays. Next to it was Neuadd Ddu Farm (taken down in the early 1980s) and, on the main road, a low thatched cottage called Neuadd Ddu where the dockworker-poet, James Hughes, was born in 1799 and lived until he was about three years of age. The cottage (cleared away in 1938) stood facing what is now the old village post office (closed in 2000). Today, poets Stevie Krayer and Anne Grimes live close by.

Cross the main road and walk up the steep hill, leaving all the houses behind you until you reach, on your left, a Unitarian chapel dating from 1755. The poet-priest David Davis (Dafis Castellhywel, 1745 – 1827) had his first ministry here, and bought a house in the village, Plas Bach, which is further up the hill by the Ladybird Nursery. Davis published a collection of his verse, Telyn Dewi, translated a number of English poems into Welsh (including Gray's Elegy, as well as works by Addison and Pope) and turned his parishioners into fervent supporters of the French Revolution. It's rumoured that the chapel contains a bust of Lenin, that once used to be in the chapel at Llwynrhydowen, where Dylan's great-uncle, Gwilym Marles, was the preacher. Further up the hill is St Michael's, a rare example in the area of a mid-eighteenth century church.

Now back to the real Trail. Turn right and cross the bridge. Here on your left is the entrance to the Tŷ Glyn walled garden, which is open to the public. Just wander down through the minor gate, passing first through the magical remains of an eighteenth century pinetum. The green door into the garden is then in front of you. The two acres were laid out in the eighteenth century, but fell into disrepair in the 1950s. It became a home for pigs, who enjoyed it immensely but uprooted the paths and other original features. When they left, nettles, brambles and dock arrived, followed by alder and willow, turning the garden into an overgrown wilderness. In 1997, the village began restoration, with a great deal of voluntary effort and a grant from the National Lottery.

This charming freehold residence is in perfect condition both inside and out and standing within carefully maintained grounds is claimed as one of the finer small country houses in Wales.

Built in 1876, the property is approached by a short carriage sweep from a Council road.

Within 4 miles of the coast. Both Aberystwyth and Lampeter are easily reached.

Accommodation on two floors is as follows :—

GROUND FLOOR :—ENTRANCE HALL 17 ft. 6 in. x 16 ft. 4 in. with galleried staircase, and parquet floor ; DRAWING ROOM (S. & W.) 21 ft. x 17 ft. ; STUDY (W.) 17 ft. x 15 ft. with fitted bookshelves ; DINING ROOM (S.), 21 ft. x 16 ft. ; MORNING ROOM (S.), 16 ft. x 14 ft. with fitted bookshelves ; CLOAKROOM with basin and W.C.

THE DOMESTIC OFFICES include KITCHEN with modern fitted sinks and " AGA " Cooker ; SCULLERY with modern fitted sink ; PANTRY with sink and extensive fitted cupboards ; SERVANTS' SITTING ROOM (S.) ; LARDER.

Excellent cellarage in which is the Domestic Hot Water Boiler.

FIRST FLOOR :—Approached by principal and secondary staircases. BEDROOM No. 1. (W) 17 ft. x 14 ft. with basin and excellent cupboards. BEDROOM No. 2 (S) 15 ft. x 14 ft. with basin ; BEDROOM No. 3. (S) 21 ft x 17 ft. with basin, communicating with : BEDROOM No. 4 or DRESSING ROOM (S) 15 ft. x 11 ft. with basin ; BEDROOM No. 5. (N) 13 ft x 10 ft ; BEDROOM No. 6. 15 ft x 15 ft. with basin. Shut off by a door are 2 further BEDROOMS ; 3 fitted BATHROOMS, each having bath, basin and W.C. Excellent hot and cold linen cupboards and Housemaid's cupboard. BOX ROOM.

Also on this floor is an excellent RECREATION ROOM 42 ft. x 19 ft. with separate staircase to outside with stage and heating stove.

*Auction details Tyglyn Aeron*

The Dylan Thomas Trail carries on down the road signposted to Aberarth. Stop first at the gate that looks across the farmyard of Tŷ Glyn Mansion. At the far end, you'll see a timber-framed granary on staddle-stones. It's the only example of such a structure in south-west Wales.

Follow the Aberarth road for about a mile as it swings sharply round to the right and climbs up above the valley once more. Pass Tynbedw Farm on your right and then turn left. The lane descends to a stony track which you follow downhill to a ford across the Aeron. There's a footbridge just to your right.

*Tyglyn Aeron, 1955*

*The Tyglyn Aeron farmyard as T.S. Eliot knew it*

*Neuadd Ddu Farm*

*James Hughes' birthplace: Neuadd Ddu cottage 1930s*

# Llanerchaeron: A Rural Nashville

Cross the footbridge and follow the track to Pandy Farm, where you turn right to pick up a metalled road. This takes you to Llanerchaeron Mansion, lived in by the same family for ten generations, now restored by the National Trust. On your right, the fattening Aeron swirls onwards to the sea; on your left are the wonderful farm buildings of the estate, set out in a series of cobbled courtyards, each devoted to an aspect of farming. Llanerchaeron is open on weekends, from April to the end of October, and you can see the mansion, the lake and the double-walled garden at your leisure.[1] The mansion, built by John Nash in 1794-96, cannot be seen from the road but even if the estate is closed you can still view the house from the parkland, which is open all year round. Continue down the road to a footpath, beyond the third main gate, that sneaks in-between the rhododendrons. Cross over the stile into the parkland and walk across to your left to view the house.

When you're ready, retrace your steps, ignoring the stile you came over, and head across the field for the church. You will now be crossing the site of a mediaeval village, which is being excavated during the summer months. Ignore the large double gates and follow the hedge between the field and the church, until you come to a gate that takes you back out onto the road. Immediately in front of you is Abermydr, a picturesque cottage designed in the Nash style for the estate coachman. Note the plane tree in the garden, a rare specimen for this part of Wales. Abermydr was for many years the home of the artist George Chapman.

Go back up the road to the church; here again we encounter Dewi Sant, for this is another dedicated to his mother, Non. It was rebuilt in 1798, probably under the influence of Nash, as the domed tower and Regency styling suggest. The graveyard is worth a wander: my favourite is the group of graves of "Road Contractors" which are to your left as you stand at the church doorway. Next to the church door is the grave of Mary Ashby Lewis, who died in 1917 aged 104, after living for seventy-six years at Llanerchaeron. She was a remarkable woman for her time, allowing her staff to vote in elections as they wished, and giving them a half-day off to do so. She paid overtime and sick leave, contributed to

---

[1] Thursdays-Sundays and Bank Holiday Mondays

local charities and was a patron of local schools.

The path now continues through the waymarked gate opposite the church. Cross the field and then onto the white footbridge that spans the Aeron. Follow the path round to the left, passing two ruined cottages which in Spring are surrounded by wild daffodils and primroses. At the second gate, turn left down the track and immediately enter the field opposite by the stile. Hug the right hand hedge of the field and the next, making for a gate and stile at the far end.

Go over the stile and on to the next, walking along a path above the Aeron hung over with hazel and hawthorn. Follow the sunken track. Where it becomes overgrown with bracken, go up into the field and follow it down. Cross a small stream and continue on the sunken track again, bearing right. Turn left over a stile and turn right onto the old railway track that will take you to the sea.

*Llanerchaeron from the site of the medieval village*

# Aberaeron: No Dive on the Quay

The old railway now serves as a route for walkers and cyclists, and follows the course of the Aeron. The Lampeter to Aberaeron line was opened to passenger traffic in May 1911 and closed in February 1951. All freight traffic was stopped in 1973. You might still kick up the occasional cinder, and some of the fencing along the way dates from the railway era.

If your lodgings are in the Llys Aeron guest house, look out for a green metal footbridge that crosses the river. This takes you through a field and up to the main road. Turn right for Llys Aeron. Otherwise, carry on down the track to its end, turning left where it joins a small country road. This will take you into Aberaeron. When you come to the main road, walk right for about twenty metres, cross over and walk through the park to Lovers Bridge. Cross over, turn right and follow the path along the river into the heart of the town.

Aberaeron is a fine example of a small Georgian seaside town. It has two beaches, one on either side of the harbour, but neither has much sand and this has probably saved the town from being overrun by visitors. Its planning and building began in the late eighteenth century, inspired by the Rev. Alban Thomas Gwynne Jones and his second wife, Susanna Maria. He died in 1819 and the major building was undertaken by his son Col. Gwynne from 1835 onwards. Many see Nash's influence on the architecture.

The development of the town was carefully controlled by Gwynne and builders had to adhere to his overall plan. Gwynne laid down the colours of the houses and insisted that they were to be repainted every two years with a terracotta lime wash. Larger buildings were placed at the centre and ends of the terraces to avoid monotony. The wide streets still give a feeling of space and peacefulness, even in a busy summer.

Look out for the original cobblestones in Alban Square, as well as the detail on the houses around the town – deeply marked corner stones, decorated lintels and porches. But be careful what you say about the new footbridge over the Aeron – it still inflames local passions for and against.

When H.V. Morton came here in 1932 it was raining and there wasn't a soul to be seen. He sought refuge in a pub, and there he met:

a depressing old man glooming over a pint of ale. He said that times were bad and would never get any better. He had a strange habit of saying 'Oh dear' to any remark made to him…But he could vary the meaning of his 'Oh dears'. He could make them sound pathetic, indignant, querulous, lachrymatory, confirmatory, shocked, incredulous and affirmative. He told me that Aberayron used to be a fishing port, but now the inhabitants fish instead for summer visitors…The amount of surprise which a Welshman can express in the word 'Oh' is astonishing. Some of them draw it out for seconds: 'O-o-o-o-o-o-o-o-h-h-h-h-h-h-H-H-H! That is *t-t-terrible!*' they will say about something that is neither terrible nor surprising, and the 'Oh' comes in a hushed, shocked way from the back of the throat, but rising in tone as it expresses amazement and incredulity.

Today, Aberaeron has learnt how to bait its hooks. Besides the elegant houses and squares, there's the Sea Aquarium, Honeybee Exhibition, Craft·Centre, vineyard, bookshops and cafes galore. It also has Cegin Cymru, a shop that sells Welsh produce, as well as a very good seafood restaurant, the Hive on the Quay. And there's a pub or two, most of which Dylan knew well because Aberaeron was Tommy Herbert's home town. Dylan's unofficial chauffeur, Dewi Ianthe, also lived here, repairing radios in a little shop that is now the Ydfa health food store.

Dylan never forgot his time in Cardiganshire: there's even a work sheet of his in the University of Texas in which he mentions "Aberayron". He lists "Newquay" as well, though today it's known as New Quay, or Cei Newydd in Welsh, and that's where the Trail takes us next.

# Along the Dolphined Coast: Aberaeron to Llanina

**6 miles**

OS Landranger Maps 146 and 145 Explorer 198

This section of the Trail starts at South Beach. You can get there by walking down Belle Vue Terrace, where Tommy Herbert lived. You'll also pass the family home of the opera singer, the late Sir Geraint Evans.

Bear left away from the yacht club, following the road past the public lavatories. You'll find the path squeezed in between the front wall of the end bungalow and the stony beach. You need to walk up into the field, ignoring the more defined path that goes straight ahead along the beach. Walk along the field edge, with the new Town Hall on your left, followed soon after by Pencarreg Morfa, a whimsical architectural collation that locals refer to as Aberaeron's Portmeirion.

The path is now easy to follow along the cliffs, crossing a number of stiles and a footbridge, eventually joining a grassy path that takes you to the waterfall at Cwm Clifforch. If you were to follow the river inland, you'd come to Henfynyw, said to be the place where Dewi Sant was educated.

Climb out up a ladder of wooden steps and cross the stile to follow the cliff edge round. Pause here to look across at New Quay head. The rock below is called Carreg Walltog, probably the inspiration for Heron Head in *Under Milk Wood*. Carreg Walltog means Hairy Rock because it's crowned with earth and grass and from the sea it looks like a man's head. But why does Dylan call it Heron Head? In a typical Dylan word play, Hair Rock becomes Hair-on-Head.

Now's the time to start looking out for dolphins, seals and porpoises. There are also choughs and peregrines to be seen, as well as the occasional swan taking the sea water. The holiday village of Gilfach yr Halen is ahead of you, a curious mix of old farmhouse buildings and modern chalets. After crossing the next stile,

*Bridge over the Drwyi*

*Llanina Point and New Quay ahead*

turn left to walk up the steep slope, staying in the open (don't enter the gorse). Where the gorse turns sharply left, carry straight on to the brow of the hill, and then descend to a stile in the corner of the field. Turn right onto the road.

Go straight through the village, climbing up past the playground and stables to a track, with more fine views of Snowdonia behind you. As you pass through a couple of gates, look out for the old stone and slate stiles. Keep on the track for about 200 metres until the waymarked path enters a field, which you need to cross diagonally to the opposite corner, until you feel you're about to drop off the edge of the world. Pause at the stile. New Quay is now clearly ahead of you. The first beach is Cei Bach and beyond it, hidden by Llanina Point, is Traethgwyn, where Caitlin liked to bathe in "the roaring ocean".

Carry on along the cliff edge to a waterfall where the river Drwyi meets the sea. There couldn't be a better place to picnic or to rest. When you climb out, be sure to take the stile into the field, and follow the green track along the bracken slopes. You'll eventually come to a wooden gate and stile. The path, roofed over with ash and hawthorn beaten flat by the south-westerlies, takes you gradually down through an avenue of gorse. Caught here between blue sky and sea, it's easy to feel that you could simply soar across to New Quay head.

The way forward, however, is more pedestrian. Go on through another wooden gate, remembering to look down to Cei Bach beach to assess the state of the tide. You'll come to a point where the path crosses with another. If the tide seems low enough to walk across the beach, turn right to zig-zag down to

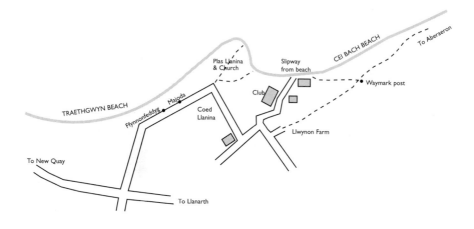

the sands. If the tide is too high, carry straight on following the waymark post, and use the high tide route described on page 83.

Once on the beach, go left, unless you fancy a bit of nude bathing, in which case you should go right to the naturist beach. Mind you, it's such a cold and windy spot that you'll need a fur coat if you're going to sunbathe.

Cei Bach, like all the beaches around New Quay, was notorious for smuggling. Wreckers also worked this stretch of coast, using lanterns and torches to lure ships onto the rocks, then plundering their cargoes to sell at the inland markets. Brigs and schooners were once built on the beach at Cei Bach. There were also lime kilns here and fishermen's cottages, now all washed away by the sea. *Siani Pob Man* (Jane Everywhere) lived here with her chickens. When the south Wales miners came on their annual holidays, she told their fortunes for a penny and sold them seaweed-tasting eggs, stained brown to make them look more attractive.

Leave the beach and ascend the concrete slipway. Follow the road round past the country club to a junction where you turn right. Go downhill for a few hundred yards, bearing to the right at the bottom. This beautiful, winding lane will take you down to Llanina, to the bridge over the river Llethi.

*Making tracks for the nudist beach, Cei Bach*

# Bullets and Lovers:
# Llanina to Goosegog Lane

**1 mile**

OS Landranger Map 145 Explorer 198

It's worth pausing on the bridge and taking stock. Upstream, you'll see Coed
Llanina, laid out in circular walks, including one that is suitable for wheelchairs.
On the other side is a mansion called Plas Llanina and the church of St. Ina, both
surrounded by woodland and the sea.

Dylan Thomas first came here in the late 1930s, in the company of Augustus
John, who brought him to meet Lord Howard de Walden. Dylan didn't just
come for the scenery or convivial company. De Walden was a major patron of
the arts in Wales and within a year he was sending money to Dylan. He also
allowed Dylan to write in the Apple House, a small stone cottage at the bottom
of the mansion's walled garden. Dylan came and worked here at various times
during the early 1940s.

Walk through the gates into Plas Llanina. The path to your right goes to the
beach but ignore it for the moment. Go straight ahead towards the house, on a
public right of way through the wooden gate. Continue up to the house,
veering right through the arched entrance way to the graveyard and church of
St. Ina.

Time now for another pause to look back at the house. Look carefully. Most
of what you see is barely ten years old, but it's a faithful reconstruction of the
original mansion built in the seventeenth century. Plas Llanina is thought to have
once been part of a village that fell into the sea as a result of erosion. The
mansion itself had a different fate: a leisure company bought it in the 1960s.
They wanted to turn the house into a casino and the fields along the cliff into a
caravan park. The caravans duly arrived but the casino proposal fell through. The
house was left to the mercy of the elements, which had none. Vandals and
builders stripped out its fine features. By the late 1980s, it was a pile of rubble,

but in the last few years it has been completely rebuilt.

As you walk down the path towards the church, look out for the second grave on your right, that of Birsha and Kathleen Davies. They were de Walden's handyman and housekeeper. Kathleen is said to have burnt a good deal of material relating to Dylan's time at Llanina. She strongly disapproved of him because, they say locally, he had made one, if not several, passes at her. There are many other interesting graves here, including those of retired sea captains, reflecting New Quay's maritime history. Some of these graves are empty because the men died at sea or in foreign ports.

There were probably two churches here before the present one, both lost to the sea, together with their graveyards. Today's church, one of the smallest in Ceredigion, was built in the 1850s, using materials from the previous church and from shipwrecks. Its dedication is not wholly clear. Some say it was dedicated to King Ina of Wessex, who was shipwrecked off the coast and saved by local villagers, who cared for him so well that he built the first church here in the eighth century. Others say the church is dedicated to Ina, Dewi Sant's aunt.

Walk across to the low wall opposite the church door and follow it back towards the house. You'll see a ruined chapel on your right, built for the private

*The chapel, Plas Llanina, used by Augustus John as a studio*

devotions of the family of the mansion. When de Walden lived here, he allowed Augustus John to use it as a makeshift studio. Before leaving the graveyard, go to the very edge of the cliff, and see what the tide is doing. You'll need this information to plan your route from Llanina into New Quay.

Dylan's time at Llanina is reflected in the first section of *Under Milk Wood*, which opens with the voices of the "long drowned" sailors. Indeed, Dylan expert John Ackerman believes that the story of Llanina's drowned cemetery "is the literal truth that inspired the imaginative and poetic truth" of the play. Dylan also appears to draw on Llanina in his poem *Ballad of the Long-legged Bait*, written in early 1941. He seems to refer to the old village of Llanina, together with its graveyard, church and fields that had been washed out to sea, in several of its verses.

## Majoda: Shot through with Rumour

Walk back now to the road and turn right up the hill. Within a few hundred yards, you'll come to Majoda, which has a plaque outside and a tree planted in the poet's memory. Dylan lived here from September 1944 to July 1945. "It's in a really wonderful bit of the bay," he wrote, "with a beach of its own. Terrific."

*Majoda*

Today, Majoda is a modern bungalow but in Dylan's time it was a wood and asbestos shack with no amenities. Dylan and his family lived here through one of the coldest winters on record, so cold that many of Cardiganshire's rivers froze. The bungalow was named after the owner's three children, Majorie, John and David. The rent was £1 a week, with calor gas for light and cooking, heating by paraffin stoves, and water from a tap on the road. Caitlin called the place "cheaply primitive". They were short of money, too, and Dylan complained he had nothing to "buy a pair of trousers, though my bum is bare to the sun".

But Dylan was happy here, and it showed in his work: he completed seven major poems, as well as *Quite Early One Morning* and a number of film scripts. Dylan also started to write *Under Milk Wood* at Majoda, and, as we shall see, he drew upon New Quay for the names of many of the characters and places in the play. It was one of the most productive periods of his adult life, a second flowering, said his biographer FitzGibbon, with a "great outpouring of poems".

*Welsh Blacks in the field next to Majoda, 1956*

Those of you intrigued with the derivation of the name "Milk Wood" should know that Majoda was surrounded by grazing cows and Dylan refers to their mooing in a May 1945 letter. The fields belonged to the Llanina estate and Howard de Walden rented them out to a local farmer. There's more on the "cows-and-woods" theory in the section on New Quay.

Carry on up the road to the next house, just a hundred metres from Majoda. This is Ffynnonfeddyg, today a Mediterranean-style villa offering five-star accommodation. In Dylan's time, it was made, like Majoda, of wood and asbestos, and built in 1932 by a local shipwright. There had once been a thatched farmhouse on the site which fell into ruin after its roof collapsed. There used to be orchards on both the sea and road sides of Ffynnonfeddyg; the 'healing well', from which the house took its name, has collapsed into the beach.

Vera and William Killick lived here, having moved across from Gelli, Talsarn. William was a commando in the SOE and in 1943 he flew into Greece to

*The "cliff-perched" town from Ffynnonfeddyg*

fight with partisans behind enemy lines. He was a courageous and heroic soldier. When he returned to New Quay in early 1945, he found that Vera had been using his army pay to support Dylan and Caitlin. Relations with Dylan became strained and a fight broke out in the Black Lion in New Quay, after Killick thought he had been slighted by Dylan and his party of film makers from London.

Killick decided to give them a taste of the war. He collected a machine gun and hand grenade from Ffynnonfeddyg and marched down to Majoda, where he fired into the bungalow. He was later arrested, tried for attempted murder and acquitted. When the trial was over, Dylan left Majoda. It's thought that both *Fern Hill* and *In my craft or sullen art* were conceived, and perhaps started, in the months at Majoda after the shooting.

New Quay locals will describe the shooting incident with a thousand embellishments, most involving sex of one kind or another. Enjoy them, but preferably with a large pinch of salt. The facts of the shooting are laid out in my previous book, using Killick's own account of his war experiences and drawing upon SOE files. There's also an internal plan of Majoda at the end of this guide, with new information about how the shooting took place.

Dylan had a number of routes for walking into New Quay from Majoda, depending on the tide and the weather. If you thought the tide was too high when you looked at it from Llanina church, carry on up past Ffynnonfeddyg to the main road, as described on page 83. If you feel happy with doing Dylan's beach route, which is by far the pleasanter option, retrace your steps to Plas Llanina. Enter the gates once more and turn right to take the footpath down to the beach. Climb the concrete steps and turn left for a bracing walk to New Quay. It will be much easier if there's sand to walk on, but if the tide's too high for that, you can pick your way along the pebbles.

## Traethgwyn Beach

Just one 150 years ago, this beach was the centre of a flourishing shipbuilding industry. The ships traded across the world, sailing to the Mediterranean, the Far East, the West Indies and South America, taking coal and iron out and returning with copper ore, nitrates, grain, hides, coffee and sugar. New Quay sailors continued to enter the merchant marine until the late 1940s, many working tankers for the oil companies. The sailors of Llareggub[2] reflect this ocean-going history of New Quay mariners, and in *Milk Wood* Dylan has them bringing home coconuts, shawls and parrots for their wives.

The beach has always been popular for its safe bathing, though one early guide warned that:

> There are no bathing machines, bathers generally bring their own tents, or, as is often the case, disrobing in the open, at various points allocated by custom to the two sexes. Mixed bathing is allowed.

About 100 metres along the beach, look up to the cliff top. Just visible in the undergrowth is the old Llanina watch tower, where Dylan sometimes worked on his poetry. Another 500 metres brings you to a pronounced cleft in the cliff, with a stream running down. You can just see the red-tiled roof of the Ffynnonfeddyg beach gate on the left. Dylan used to walk from Majoda across the cliff, take the path down from Ffynnonfeddyg, jump across the stream and climb up the other side to carry on to New Quay. This path has now disappeared because of erosion so we need to carry on along the beach, as Dylan sometimes did.

Ahead is New Quay. In his radio broadcast, *The Crumbs of One Man's Year*, Dylan described this walk from Majoda under:

> the flayed and flailing cliff-top trees, when the wind played old Harry, or old Thomas, with me, and cormorants, far off, sped like motor-boats across the bay, as I weaved towards the toppling town and the black, loud *Lion* where the cat, who purred like a fire, looked out of two cinders at the gently swilling retired sea-captains in the snug-as-a-bug back bar.

Here on the beach, watching the town slide down into the bay, you can see how the poet's imagination worked when he described Llareggub as a "hill of windows". Think, too, of the Voice of a Guide Book in *Under Milk Wood*, which describes Llareggub as consisting:

---

[2] Llareggub is the name of the town in *Under Milk Wood*

for the most part, of humble, two-storied houses many of which attempt to achieve some measure of gaiety by prinking themselves out in crude colours and by the liberal use of pinkwash.

Head for the white house, about half-way along the beach, on the cliff edge. Ignore the concrete steps that come after the white house. Look out for a dirt and stone path up from the beach, just a few yards after the large wooden piles that stand out prominently from the sand like giant sponge fingers. The path is guarded by some large boulders to stop erosion but the bottom is usually washed away.

Take the path up and, almost immediately, go right at the first junction, through a beautiful glade of harts-tongue ferns. Go past the first house, Traethina, and a white bungalow, around which the path sweeps upwards to a

*"did a jig on the Llanina sands"*

waymark post. Turn right up the steps for New Quay and carry on past the caravans to a handsome cottage called Brongwyn. The path now broadens out into Brongwyn Lane, a walk once much-favoured by courting couples, and probably the inspiration for Goosegog Lane in *Under Milk Wood*. On the right in Dylan's time was Maesgwyn Farm, a name he uses in the opening part of the play as the drowned sailors reminisce with Captain Cat. The farmhouse, fields and chestnut trees have long since disappeared beneath the waves. Indeed, there was once a little community up here, Pentre Siswrn, but it, two roads and about sixty acres of good farmland have been lost to the sea. It is these drowned houses and fields that inspire "the imaginative and poetic truth" of *Under Milk Wood* as much as those of Llanina. Not to mention the 150 sailors in local graveyards who died at sea or in foreign ports.

Carry on to the top of Brongwyn Lane. Here stood a house called Sunnydale, proud and well-appointed until the night the sea took away its foundations. Skipper Rymer lived here, once a trawler man with Neal and West, a hard man at sea, a thirsty one ashore, distinguished by the bowler hat he wore on the bridge. He ran the Dolau pub in the town for a couple of years after the war. More on him later.

Pause at the junction with the main road that will take you into New Quay, first along George Street and then Margaret Street (Stryd Bethel).

# Dylan's New Quay: a street-wise poem...

Dear Tommy, please, from far, sciatic Kingsley
Borrow my eyes. The darkening sea flings Lee
And Perrins on the cockled tablecloth
Of mud and sand. And, like a sable moth,
A cloud against the glassy sun flutters his
Wings. It would be better if the shutter is
Shut. Sinister dark over Cardigan
Bay. No-good is abroad. I unhardy can
Hardly bear the din of No-good wracked dry on
The pebbles. It is time for the Black Lion
But there is only Buckley's unfrisky
Mild. Turned again, Worthington. Never whisky.
I sit at the open window, observing
The salty scene and my Playered gob curving
Down to the wild, umbrella'd, and french-lettered
Beach, hearing rise slimy from the Welsh lechered
Caves the cries of the parchs and their flocks. I
Hear their laughter sly as gonococci...
There slinks a snoop in black. I'm thinking it
Is Mr Jones the Cake, that winking-bit,
That hymning gooseberry, that Bethel-worm
At whose ball-prying even death'll squirm
And button up. He minces among knickers,
That prince of pimps, that doyen of dung-lickers.
Over a rump on the clerical-grey seashore,
See how he stumbles. Hallelujah hee-haw!
His head's in a nest where no bird lays her egg.
He cuts himself on an elder's razor leg.
Sniff, here is sin! Now must he grapple, rise:
He snuggles deep among the chapel thighs,
And when the moist collection plate is passed
Puts in his penny, generous at last.

Part of a letter/poem sent to Tommy Earp from Majoda, September 1944,
*Collected Letters.*

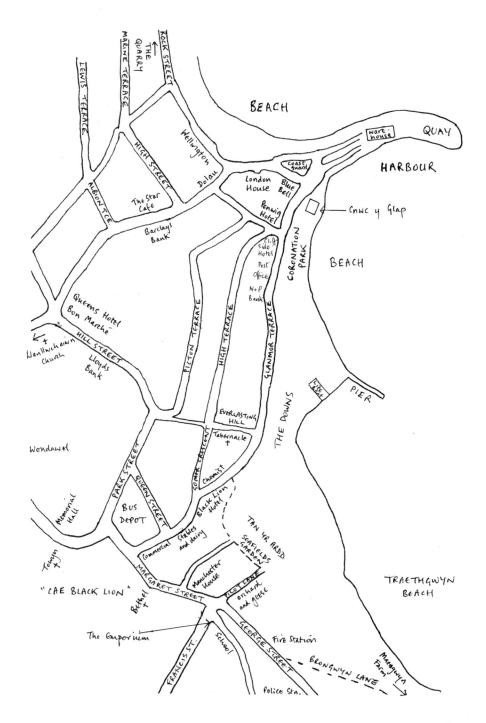

BEACH

QUAY

HARBOUR

ware-house

coast guard

LEWIS TERRACE

MARINE TERRACE

THE QUARRY

ROCK STREET

HIGH STREET

Wellington

Dolau

London House

Blue Bell

Penwig Hotel

Cnwc y Glap

ALBION TCE

The Star Cafe

Barclays Bank

Cliff Side Hotel

Post Office

N & P Bank

CORONATION PARK

BEACH

Queens Hotel Bon Marché

Hanllwchairn Church

HILL STREET

Lloyds Bank

PICTON TERRACE

HIGH TERRACE

SLANMOR TERRACE

PIER

Life Boat

THE DOWNS

EVERLASTING HILL

Tabernacle

Wendawel

PARK STREET

QUEEN STREET

SOBAR CRESCENT

Chemist

Memorial Hall

BUS DEPOT

Black Lion Hotel

Towyn

Commercial

Stables and dairy

TAN YR ARDD

SEAFIELDS GARDEN

TRAETHGWYN BEACH

"CAE BLACK LION"

MARGARET STREET

Bethel

Manchester House

PLOU LANE

orchard and geese

The Emporium

FRANCIS ST

School

GEORGE STREET

Fire Station

BRONGWYN LANE

Maesgwyn Farm

Police Stn.

51

# Polly Garter's New Quay: Meeting the People of *Under Milk Wood*

**1 mile**

OS Landranger 145, Explorer 198

Stand on this spot. This is New Road, old as the hills, high, wet and green, and from this small resting place next to the undertakers, you can see the town below you. You can hear the love-sick teenagers mooning in their caravans. Dogs bark to earn their keep, farmyards away. New Quay ripples...

**Voice of A Rough Guide Book**

Along with Laugharne, **New Quay** lays claim to being the original Llareggub in Dylan Thomas' *Under Milk Wood*. Certainly, it has the little tumbling streets, prim Victorian terraces, cobblestone harbour, pubs and dreamy isolation that Thomas so successfully invoked in his play. In the height of the tourist season, however, the quiet seclusion can be hard to find, although even at these times, the town maintains a charm lost in so many other Ceredigion resorts. Although there is a singular lack of excitement in New Quay, it does make a great base for coastal walks and the odd boat trip...The main road cuts through the upper, residential part of the town, past Uplands square, from where acutely inclined streets swoop down to the pretty **harbour**, formed by its sturdy stone quay, and small curving **main beach**...the higgledy-piggledy lines of multi-coloured shops and houses comprise the **lower town**, the more traditionally seaside part of New Quay, full of cafes, pubs and beach shops...**bottlenosed dolphins** are one of New Quay's major attractions, and can often be seen frolicking by the harbour wall, particularly when the tide is full and the weather calm. There are also several **boat trips** geared around potential sightings. (1998)

In Dylan's day, life in New Quay mostly revolved around chapel, music, poetry and the sea – just like Llareggub. It had its farmers and fishermen, cobblers and schoolteachers, weeded widows and tidy young wives, of course, but it was a town that also abounded with singers, writers, painters and webfooted sea captains. And it was, and largely still is, a town of terrace, wood and beach – just like Llareggub. Its "salt-white houses" dangle over the sea, squatting prim, as Dylan observed, "in neatly treed but unsteady hill streets." Welsh was widely spoken, and the town had its own distinctive dialect.

The inspiration for many of the people and places of *Under Milk Wood* can be found on Dylan's walk into, and around, New Quay, beginning here at the junction of George Street and Brongwyn Lane. As his friend Tommy Herbert said:

> Whenever he walked from Cnwc y Lili [Majoda] to the shops in Newquay, he would spend time chattering with the locals, and, I believe, partly adopted them as his characters.

Look first over your shoulder, at the dark-stoned house above the road, "black as a helmet, dry as a summons, sober as Sunday," as Dylan described it in *Quite Early One Morning*. This is the **old police station**, the Handcuff House of *Milk Wood*. It was both cophouse and home, where PC Islwyn Williams and his family lived.

Then listen to Llareggub's PC Attila Rees:

> *ox-broad, barge-booted, stomping out of Handcuff House in a heavy beef-red huff, black browed under his damp helmet…*

Was Attila Rees inspired by PC Islwyn Williams? Williams was indeed an ox-broad man, and a member of the police Ju Jitsu team. He had "big slug eyebrows," his son told me, "and he huffed and puffed like an old steam train, whatever he was doing, even the washing up." In earlier drafts of *Milk Wood*, Dylan drew even more attention to Attila Rees' eyebrows, describing them as "cross as black crabs" and as "thick as boot brushes". Dylan certainly knew the New Quay policeman: his favourite places for keeping watch on the town were

*PC Islwyn Williams, centre, on leave, late 1930s*

*PC Williams' father, John, with the distinctive family eyebrows*

55

outside the Commercial and Blue Bell pubs. And it was PC Williams who arrested William Killick, and gave evidence, along with Dylan, in Killick's trial.

Walk down George Street, full of shops in Dylan's time, including two cobblers, a grocer and a toy shop. There was also a fire station and, opposite, an old-style cottage occupied by Miss Jones Fach. Like Captain Cat, she spent her days at an open window, observing the townsfolk at work and play.

The house just before the garage was once the shop of **Thomas Shirley Brooks** the photographer, who had come to New Quay after many years of "Professional Experience in London and Provincial Studios." Perhaps Brooks inspired Dylan to describe Llareggub's Mr Pritchard as a "Photographer Elite" in an early draft of the play. Certainly, Shirley Brooks' shop window and pavement display dominated George Street, which Dylan went down every day on his way to the pub.

Stop at the corner of Margaret Street and Francis Street. Listen to...

The children in the **school playground** just across the road, hearing in your mind, as Dylan did in his, the penny-a-kiss voices of Gwennie, Billy, Dicky and Johnnie Cristo. There was a sweet shop here in Dylan's time, the **Emporium**, just like the one run in Llareggub by:

*Me, Miss Price, in my pretty print housecoat, deft at the clothesline, natty as a jenny-wren...*

Opposite is **Pilot Lane**, down which Dylan went to the back door of the Black Lion. On the right of the lane were the orchard and geese of Mrs Huw Davies, mother of Tydur, who was Dylan's regular taxi driver. Dylan mentions an orchard and goosefield in *Under Milk Wood*. As the lane turns left to the Black Lion, the garden in front of you belonged, in Dylan's time, to "Seafields", the home of Daniel the Electric. The garden was noted for its display of gooseberry bushes. Some New Quay residents think that Pilot Lane inspired Goosegog Lane because it had Mrs Huw Davies' geese and Mr Daniel's gooseberry bushes. This whole area below the Black Lion was known as Tan yr Ardd – Under the Garden.

Return now to Margaret Street. First on your right...

The showcase windows of **Manchester House**, stock full of rods and maggots, with a breath-baiting collection of hooks, lines and sinkers. But you, and only you, can see flannel and calico, bombazine, taffeta, chiffon and cashmere, tussah, cretonne, cambric, madras, paisley, ticking and cavalry twill. Dylan knew the shop as a draper's, the kind that Mog Edwards had in *Milk Wood* where the change hummed along wires.

---

### D. E. THOMAS
Established 1804.            (Late Wm. JAMES).
*General Draper & Milliner*
**MANCHESTER HOUSE, NEW QUAY**

---

Next to it, the old **Sheffield House**, then the ironmonger's and general store, typical of those to be found in Welsh villages of the time. The one in Llareggub was run by Mrs Organ Morgan, selling custard and buckets, rat traps and stamps, confetti and paraffin, hatchets and whistles.

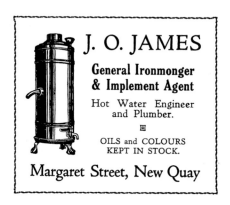

On the left side of the street, you'll find **Goytre**, where the Rev. W.O. Jenkins lived in the 1940s; Dylan may have borrowed his name for the Rev. Eli Jenkins in *Milk Wood*. A few doors down was **Brooklands** (now Eastcliffe), which was the home of Walter Cherry, town councillor, magistrate, church warden, bookmaker and one of Dylan's drinking companions in the Black Lion.[3]

---

[3] Further investigation have established that Brooklands was the present-day Eastcliffe, not Clarita.

His son-in-law was Dan 'Cherry' Jones, who gave his name to Cherry Owen, the loveable old soak of *Milk Wood* who reeled in:

> *as drunk as a deacon with a big wet bucket and a fish-frail full of stout...*
> *sprawling and bawling, and the floor was all flagons and eels...*

Dylan inadvertently uses the name "Cherry Jones" in one of his drafts of the play. Furthermore, in an early list of *Milk Wood* characters, Dylan describes Cherry Owen as a plumber and carpenter – Cherry Jones was a general builder. There couldn't be a more convincing example of the way in which Dylan drew on New Quay people and places for the play.

```
┌─────────────────────────────────────────┐
│  D. J. JONES :  BUILDER AND              │
│                 CONTRACTOR.              │
│      All Work Personally Supervised.     │
│                                          │
│  BROOKLANDS   ::   NEW QUAY              │
└─────────────────────────────────────────┘
```

Come now, tie up your nightshirt and drift down to the terraced end of the sea-bright street to...

**Maglona**, that used to be a barber's shop. Next door, **Arnant**, Glanmor Rees' cobbler's shop, also selling delicious lettuces and small shrimping nets, as a writer in *The Lady* noticed, on a visit in 1959 to this town that he thought was "another *Milk Wood*." In his back room, Rees, the town's philosopher cobbler, presided over his tobacco parliament, where

> *Alfred Pomeroy Jones, sealawyer, born in Mumbles,*

would have felt at home arguing the toss. Dylan also liked to sit here, with Lord Howard de Walden, gossiping with the old sailors, no doubt sizing up Mr Rees as Jack Black the cobbler who chased the courting couples down Brongwyn Lane, *driving out the bare, bold girls from the sixpenny hops of his nightmares.*

Next door is **Bethel** chapel. Dylan sometimes used "Bethel" to express his disapproval of hypocrisy but in *Milk Wood* he turned Bethel into the more benign Bethesda. On the other side of the chapel was Mr John's bakery,

**The Cake Shop**. There is no suggestion that Mr John had two wives like

*Me, Dai Bread, hurrying to the bakery, pushing in my shirt-tails, buttoning my*
*waistcoat, ping goes a button, why can't they sew them, no time for breakfast,*
*nothing for breakfast, there's wives for you...*

Mr John was both baker and aquatic stuntman, and he appears as Mr Jones the Cake in Dylan's New Quay poem. (The original bakery was burnt down in a fire and replaced by the present Costcutter shop.)

---

## E. C. JOHN

High-class **Baker & Confectioner**

HOVIS, TUROG & SPECIAL
WHOLE-MEAL BREAD
CAKES AND PASTRIES
*Tea Gardens and Café on Front*

—

**The Cake Shop, New Quay**

---

Opposite The Cake Shop was **Compton House** (now the New Quay Football Club). It was once a bed and breakfast and, at pavement level, a chemist shop, full of weedkiller, arsenic and digestive tablets big as horse-pills, where Mr Pugh, school teacher

*minces among bad vats and jeroboams, tiptoes through spinneys of murdering*
*herbs...and mixes especially for Mrs Pugh a venomous porridge unknown to*
*toxologists which will scald and viper through her until her ears fall off like figs, her*
*toes grow big and black as balloons, and steam comes screaming out of her navel.*

Here, where Margaret Street turns into Glanmor Terrace, stood the **Commercial**, now the Seahorse. It was once called the Sailor's Home Arms, and was certainly the inspiration for the name of Llareggub's pub, the Sailors' Arms. In Dylan's day, there were two entrances, one on the corner where the extractor fan is now. There were a pair of swing doors here, which led into a small bar with a piano on the right-hand side; in the back room, there were "two very large & very fine coloured prints of Louis Wain cats," as Dylan once described in a letter about New Quay.

Jon Meirion Jones, the biographer of the Cilie poets, remembers passing the Commercial as a schoolboy, and hearing some strange but wonderful music being played. He pushed open the swing doors and looked inside. There was Dill Jones playing jazz on the piano, with Dylan at the table next to him. It was early summer, 1946, almost a year after Dylan had left Majoda. There's more about this on page 102, as well as a brief biography of Dill Jones on page 137.

The large car park that now dominates this part of the town used to be small fields, with hedges and trees. They were part of "Cae Black Lion", fields where Dylan's good friend Jack Patrick of the Black Lion kept his cows. They were driven down through the streets for milking in his dairy (now an amusement arcade) next to the pub. This may be another inspiration for the name "Milk Wood". Note, too, that New Quay was known, as the *Welsh Gazette* tells us, for its "abundance" of hazel copses "with their crops of milky nuts." The town was thus well and truly under its own milk woods.

The windows of the town lighten now. The Rev. Eli Jenkins

> *...gropes out of bed into his preacher's black, combs back his bard's white hair, forgets to wash, pads barefoot downstairs, opens his front door, stands in the doorway and, looking out at the day and up at the eternal hill, and hearing the sea break and the gab of birds, remembers his own verses and tells them, softly, to empty Coronation Street that is rising and raising its blinds.*

But wait. Listen. You alone can hear the strictly metred verses of...

The Rev. Orchwy Bowen of **Towyn**, the chapel that stands proud above the car park, within sinning distance of the Seahorse. Bowen was a preacher-poet and, like Eli Jenkins, he also had bardic white hair and was a familiar figure about the town in Dylan's day. He published his poetry and was a regular competitor in the county eisteddfodau. His sons Geraint and Euros won the Chair and Crown in post-war National Eisteddfodau. Could Dylan have had a better model for Eli Jenkins?

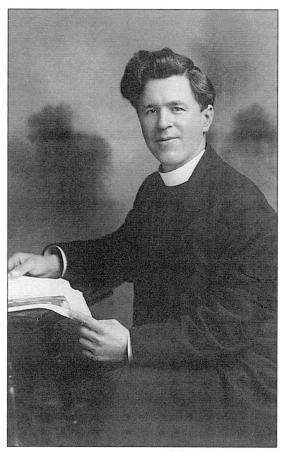

*Orchwy Bowen (1882-1948)*

Across the road from Towyn is the **Memorial Hall**, recalling the Welfare Hall in Llareggub whose floors were scrubbed by

> *Me, Polly Garter, under the washing line, giving the breast in the garden to my bonny new baby. Nothing grows in our garden, only washing. And babies.*

The Hall was one of the centres of New Quay's cultural life during the 1930s and 1940s. Here were staged plays, concerts, eisteddfodau and operettas, put on by the townspeople themselves or by touring companies.

A GRAND

# Variety

## Entertainment

*in aid of the*

# SPITFIRE

# FUND

*Behold these bri*

*beings so brimful*

*bliss. What is the*

*Wherefore those se*

*on the strac*

*the ridd*

*to a n*

*Peace shall reign once more. They are ourselves,*

*destruction upon the heads of those who seek to cr*

Inan Jouss
Nov. 1940

ill be held at the MEMORIAL HALL on
WEDNESDAY, NOV. 20th?

Chairman : W.A. Price, Esq.

ADMISSION

Reserved Seats : 2/-

Other Seats :
1/6 & 1/-

Doors open – 7 o'clock    To commence – 7.30

Tickets at the LION HOTEL
and ANGORFA

of their joy?
smiles? Look up and you will see, blazoned
re, the announcement wherin lies the answer to
ey are looking forward with serene confidence
first-class entertainment and to the Day when
friends, each of us doing his share in hurling
. Crush us? They would if they could, but can they? NOT—LIKELY!!

Designed by
Ieuan Jones
'Adpar', 1940

Curl up your toes now, and fall down Glanmor Terrace to…

**Rosehill**, opposite the not-so-funny amusement arcade. This was the home of Captain Charles Patrick, known locally as Captain Pat, and uncle of Jack Pat of the **Black Lion**, which is now in front of you as you look down towards the sea. The Lion used to be Dylan's favourite pub, and the restaurant today has a marvellous collection of photographs of Dylan and other memorabilia. It was here that Dylan listened to the gossip of the town, rich material for *Under Milk Wood*, as Jack Pat has described: "He was just interested in people, any character at all, and listened to them, and busy with his notes at all times."

There's a reference at the beginning of *Milk Wood* to "buttermilk and whippets"; Jack Pat bred whippets and made buttermilk in the Black Lion dairy.

See, now, **Gomer House**, opposite the hotel, within latch-lifting reach of the public bar. This was the home of Captain Tom Davies, universally known as Tom Polly, after the name of his boat. He was a retired master mariner, and another drinking companion of Dylan's in the Black Lion. Was Tom Polly the inspiration for

*Captain Cat, the retired blind seacaptain, asleep in his bunk in the seashelled, ship-in-bottled, shipshape best cabin of Schooner House…*

Certainly, Tom Polly was well-known for standing outside his house watching the people walking back and forth to the harbour, just as Captain Cat sat in his home listening to the comings and goings of Llareggub. Moreover, Tom Polly had worked as a censor for part of the war, and had been a Government Observer during the Spanish Civil War. Both these roles probably helped to form Dylan's image of Captain Cat as "The witness", as Dylan described him in a list of the characters of the play, someone privy to the everyday lives and secrets of the people of Llareggub.

*What seas did you see,*
*Tom Cat, Tom Cat,*
*In your sailoring days*
*Long long ago?*

And whilst Captain Cat lived in Schooner House, Tom Polly lived in Schooner Town. Ninety-nine schooners were built or owned in New Quay between 1848 and 1870 – as well as over a hundred barques, brigantines and smacks.

Today, the shop opposite the public bar of the Black Lion sells ice cream, novelties and toys. In Dylan's time, it was the shop of Mr Harries the Chemist, also Special Constable, in charge of law and order at the Women's Institute's social dances in the Memorial Hall, making sure that no un-wedding-ringed Polly Garter slipped in. Busy making his fortune in stocks and shares, Mr Harries didn't really want customers disturbing his calculations, and when he did serve, the potions and pills were always wrapped in the *Financial Times*.

Keep on the right side of Glanmor Terrace, and note the area of steep grassland (now landscaped but once rough pasture) that sweeps down from the Black Lion to the

*Tom Polly, right, in Barcelona, 1938*

Lifeboat Station, where once stood cottages known as the **Downs**. Jack Pat grazed his donkeys here, and it may have inspired Llareggub's Donkey Down.

To your right is the sweep of Cardigan Bay and the coast you've just walked along, with "the splashed church" of Llanina at the far end of the wild, unparasoled beach. In front of you on the **harbour**, the "empty but for rats and whispers grey warehouse", with the more modern New Quay yacht club anchored to its side like a limpet. The protective arm of "the **quay** shouldering out" cradles the pleasure-boat-bobbing sea. These are the boats that will take you chugging past the caves in which, according to Dylan, you can see the elders snuggling deep among the chapel thighs. Indeed, one of them is called Parson's Cave.

*The whispering warehouse and the shouldering quay, c. 1936*

Ice cream bells chime, gulls heckle and children whine. But if you listen carefully, you can hear, from where you are, an old man playing the harmonium:

*Oh, Bach without any doubt. Bach every time for me.*

The age-old ghost of Organ Morgan plays in **Tabernacle** chapel, next to you, on your left. It was one of the important centres of music-making in Dylan's New Quay, and almost every night some concert or rehearsal would fill the night air with full-throated Welsh singing, amplified in the double catch of the bay and the town's hills. The effect would have been very pronounced on Sundays because the three chapels, clustered together at the top of the town, began their morning and evening services at the same time – as did the church. No wonder that in Llareggub *the music of the spheres is heard distinctly over Milk Wood.*

The lane next to the chapel that takes you back up to the top of the town was known as Everlasting Hill, recalling Llareggub's "eternal hill" that Eli Jenkins looks up to as he starts his morning poem.

Time's passing.

Wind royally down to the trees of **Coronation Park**, past Craig-y-Môr and Glan-y-Don, Morawel and Pencraig; past *curtained fernpot, text and trinket, harmonium, holy dresser, watercolours done by hand, china dog and rosy tin caddy*; past the National and Provincial Bank to...

The **Post Office,** now the Hungry Trout restaurant, from where Dylan sent his telegrams and scripts to London. Jack Lloyd was one of the postal workers, and Dylan knew him well, drawing on him for the character of Willy Nilly, Llareggub's postman. Lloyd was also New Quay's Town Crier. Willy Nilly's penchant for opening letters, and spreading the town's news from one house to another, is a strong reflection of Lloyd's role as Crier, as Dylan himself noted on one of his drafts of *Under Milk Wood*. (The name Willy Nilly probably came from Will and Lil Evans, who were the town's other postal workers.)

A few doors down were the Cliffside Hotel and the **Hotel Penwig**. During the war, this were one of the centres of New Quay's active and varied sex life, as I've described in my previous book. There was more than enough happening in New Quay to provide Dylan with a wealth of material for his description of the lustings and couplings of the people of Llareggub.


Go closer now to...

The sea-washed **Blue Bell** on the bottom corner, where PC Williams stood like a capstan on even the wildest nights. It's a rather different pub today to the one that Dylan knew, and where he sometimes drank with the young Richard Burton. Then it was the favourite of the boys from the boats, who hosed themselves down on the flag floor when they needed to sober up. The landlady was Auntie Cat (Catrin), a name like those of Captain Pat and Jack Pat, that may have inspired the name of Captain Cat.

Across the road, squat but commodious, conveniences for the public, hot and cold running, silent flushing, no cold draughts. In Dylan's time, it was the old life-boat station, the daily meeting place – **Cnwc y Glap** – of the retired sea captains and their mates, an occasion to reminisce and recall old friends, as only you can hear:

*First Drowned: Remember me, Captain?*

*Second Drowned: Is there rum and laverbread?*

*Third Drowned: How's the tenors in Dowlais?*

*Fourth Drowned: Ebenezer's bell?*

There were over thirty-five retired, ocean-going captains in New Quay when Dylan was there – a wonderful gallery of Captain Cats to inspire his imagination! It's made clear in *Milk Wood* that Captain Cat was a well-travelled man who had seen the world. As such, he is rooted at the centre of New Quay's economic and cultural life – of the master mariners listed in Kelly's trade directories for south Wales, almost sixty percent came from the coastal towns of Cardiganshire, and the majority of these were from New Quay. In the 1930s, one in five of New Quay's men aged twenty and over were master mariners, either retired or serving.

Cnwc y Glap certainly inspired the young boys of the Cilie family, who came often to listen to the sea captains' talk. Indeed, both Alun Cilie and Simon Cilie referred to Cnwc y Glap in their poems, and Simon won the 1933 Crown at the National Eisteddfod with his poem *Round the Horn*. One visitor was so impressed with Cnwc y Glap, he wrote that it was "the only public institution, where it seems matters of all kinds are discussed. Yarns are spun, as well as political questions of the utmost gravity handled."

Go closer still now, past the milk bar, cafes and chip 'n' bottled take-aways, past the sea-front teashop full of "large, straight-backed, prim-faced matrons in black bombazine, alarming hats mantled with fruit and flowers" that writer Reginald Thompson found himself wedged between on his visit in 1936, to…

**London House.** In Dylan's day, it was a grocer's shop where his friend Norman Evans worked, when he wasn't hanging around the harbour doing odd jobs on the boats, although, said one resident, "you never actually *saw* Norman working." Norman, whose own boat was aptly called the *Idle Hour*, was a lazy and drunken fisherman, who liked nothing better than dawdling "away the rodless day", as Dylan described Boyo in an early draft of *Milk Wood*. But

*Visitors drowse angelically in Coronation Park. Behind them, from left to right, the National and Provincial Bank; the Post Office; Araminta; Parana; Cliffside Hotel; Hotel Penwig; the old Sail Loft; and, in its shadow, the two-storied Blue Bell with, opposite, Cnwc y Glap, on top of the rocks; with the whispering, grey warehouse on the far right. c. 1948*

*Colliers from south Wales on holiday at New Quay, c. 1910*

Norman was an accomplished *all-round* no-gooder: he was, as Dylan once observed, "New Quay's least successful street fighter." He was also an incompetent shopkeeper, and often up to no good in the bedrooms of the Penwig Hotel. Yet everybody had a soft spot for him, not least because – like Dylan – he was always breaking his bones.[4] So look carefully now, and you can see

*Me, Nogood Boyo, up to no good in the wash-house…*

Continue on now, past trinket shops and tourist office, swamped by the big seas of holiday dreams, past chip shop and booted pub, a much smaller wellington in Dylan's time, past the not so dab-filled sea, along Rock Street to find Llareggub's Mr Waldo carrying on with that Mrs Beattie Morris up in the quarry.

New Quay's **quarry** provided much of the stone for building the town. It was also used for picnicking, impromptu concerts and love-making, as one contributor to the *New Quay Chronicle* noted:

> Should Cupid pierce the tender hearts of the lovely maidens and brave young men, the quarry and the lonely cliffs form an unapproachable fortress to guard their faltering confessings.

The quarry's manager was Evan Joshua James. He drank in the Black Lion and Blue Bell with Dylan. He was a creative and well-read man, wrote short stories and contributed articles on the town to the *Welsh Gazette*. He was a New Quay boy, who had worked in Dowlais and Swansea before returning to New Quay. Whilst working in Swansea, Evan Joshua lived in the St Thomas district, and came to know several members of the Williams family, Dylan's maternal aunts and uncles.

Go back now to the tourist office and turn into Church Street. Skipper Rymer's **Dolau** looks invitingly down on you. It was Caitlin's favourite New

---

[4] Dylan's notes on Nogood Boyo read: "Odd job man, loathes all jobs. Won't go to church, work, vote, wash. Fishes sometimes. Is supported, often, by those who disapprove of him."

*Evan Joshua James, 1940s*

Quay pub. The aristocratic Alastair Graham, nephew of the Duchess of Montrose, also came here every day, and Dylan drew upon him as the model for

> *Me, Lord Cut-Glass, in an old frock-coat belonged*
> *to Eli Jenkins and a pair of postman's trousers from*
> *Bethesda Jumble…*

Graham had been Evelyn Waugh's lover, and Waugh used him as the basis for Sebastian Flyte in *Brideshead Revisited*. Graham lived on the outskirts of the town at **Plas y Wern** – see page 125. Dylan sometimes went to parties there and Graham occasionally supported him with money. Other visitors at the Wern included Edward VIII, Compton Mackenzie, and Maxwell Knight, chief of counter-espionage at MI5, who shared Graham's passion for fishing.

Next to the Dolau is the Port of Call, formerly known as Dolau Uchaf, thought to be the first house in New Quay to be given a slate roof. A Chilean sailor called Valparaiso once lived here, who delighted in scaring children by showing them his back, badly disfigured by a cat o' nine tails. Welsh rugby international, Cliff Jones, owned the house in the 1950s; distinguished guests included Richard Burton and Paul Scofield.

A few yards further on, turn into High Street and walk along to **Marine Terrace**, full of old New Quay atmosphere, and the best views over Cardigan Bay. Dylan's friend, Dai Fred, lived here in 'Bayfield'; he made ships-in-bottles and carved dildoes out of wood. Dai Fred was the donkeyman on board the *Alpha*, and Dylan turned him into Llareggub's:

> *Tom-Fred the donkeyman…We shared the*
> *same girl once…Her name was Mrs Probert…*

At the end of the terrace, there's a footpath which takes you into the quarry at a higher level, with a close-up view of Carreg Walltog ("Heron Head") and a fine sense of the hewn amphitheatre in which the miners and iron workers sang their hearts out.

Higher up Church Street, on the corner opposite the curry house, was the shop of Neuadd Dairy, where butcher **Hell Fire Jones** worked, remembered even today for pursuing children down the street in mock chases, brandishing a cleaver. Perhaps this gave Dylan the idea for Llareggub's Butcher Beynon, springheeling down Coronation Street with a finger in his mouth, but not his own, chasing corgis with his cleaver.

Here, too, was **Barclay's Bank**, managed by Mr Pritchard Jones, and, at the top of the street, **Bon Marché**, formerly a draper's shop owned by Ogmore 'Tom' Davies (now a chemist's). Were their names and their wives part of the inspiration for Mrs Ogmore-Pritchard, who first appeared in Dylan's portrait of the town, *Quite Early One Morning*? Many in New Quay think so: "They were both rather snobbish, very prim." Mrs Pritchard Jones had much in common with the obsessively clean Mrs Ogmore-Pritchard: "She was well-known in the town, like her husband. I *think* she was a Queen's Nurse from North Wales, a real matron-type, very strait-laced, house-proud, ran the home like a hospital ward."

Yet we shouldn't be too harsh, for there were many Mrs Ogmore-Pritchards in New Quay. The town prided itself on its wholesome air and clean streets. An early guide noted that:

> The place has the reputation of being amongst the cleanest in the Principality. The Houses, inside and out, the Streets and Terraces and everything without exception, are kept in a state of spotless cleanliness and high polish.

If you were to walk to the top of Church Street and follow the main road to the right, you'd come to the parish church of **Llanllwchaiarn**. This again has one of those maritime cemeteries of many empty graves. Sarah Marietta is buried here, first wife of J.T. Jôb (1867–1938), another of Wales' poet-priests, and winner of the National Eisteddfod Chair three times and the Crown once.

The church bell came from St Mair's church in Dowlais when it was demolished in 1963. There was a special relationship between New Quay and Dowlais, based partly on marriage and the migration of New Quay men looking for work; furthermore, Evan Joshua James had been an overseer there, and he had encouraged the annual outings of Dowlais families to New Quay. Evan Joshua's grand-daughter, Nell Highet, remembers her parents talking about the workers "from Dowlais coming to New Quay on holiday and singing on the pier on a summer evening." It's hardly surprising then that Dylan mentions the tenors of Dowlais in the opening pages of *Under Milk Wood*, or that the special relationship with Dowlais is also reflected in the work of some of the Cilie poets who refer to the town, eg Isfoel and Sioronwy.

Opposite Llanllwchaiarn is Towyn Road. Half-way along on the right (immediately next to Bella Vista) is **Wendawel** (Pure Peace). It was built by Evan Joshua for Dylan's aunt Elizabeth Ann Williams and her daughter Theodosia, when they first came to New Quay. By the middle-to-late 1930s, Dylan was visiting New Quay, not in search of pure peace but money, as the family remembers it.

*Dylan's first cousin, Theodosia, taken by Shirley Brooks in New Quay, 1927*

Theodosia married in 1930, and her in-laws moved to New Quay in the 1940s, from St Thomas. Many other Swansea families, including Dylan's friends Vera Killick and her sister Evelyn, came to live in the town during the war. Myra Evans, whom Dylan once asked for Welsh lessons, returned to war-time New Quay from Swansea; she was the sister of Glanmor Rees the cobbler and had married Evan Jenkin Evans, the first professor of physics at Swansea. Here, perhaps, lies a clue to why Dylan seemed so contented in New Quay, and so productive: it was home-from-home, the terraces of his childhood Uplands in salty miniature, with an aunt and a cousin, and a town full of people who had been brought up in Swansea or, like Evan Joshua, had lived and worked there and known his mother's family. And New Quay people, of course, knew all about Swansea: it's where they went for special holiday treats, major medical treatment, and to welcome home their docking menfolk from the sea.

And that's it! The end of the Dylan Thomas Trail. Your walk which started in Llanon with Dewi Sant's mum has ended with Dylan's auntie who swapped Bay View, St Thomas, for the magnificent bay views of Wendawel at the very top of this trig and trimmed town.

Time now for a beer or, better still, a glass of milk to toast our patron St. Ffraed, and all those in the dairy trade whom she so faithfully protects, even Ocky Milkman watering Llareggub with his half-dew milk; even the local farmers who regularly appeared in the court reports of the *Welsh Gazette* of the 1940s, charged with adulterating their milk; even "the vendors of milk in London, with their suspected partiality for water," who, according to Watkin Davies, "have also very largely been Cardiganshire folk."

Time to reflect on how so many of Llareggub's people and places occur within the short stretch, less than a mile, between Brongwyn Lane and Church Street. Except one...

The river **Dewi**, whose song the Rev. Eli Jenkins liked to hear all day without ever, ever having to leave the town. The Dewi is just outside New Quay, entering the sea at Cwmtydu. From where you are, it's just a couple of miles' walking on the footpath at the end of Lewis Terrace.[5] This is the cliff path

---

[5] While you're in Lewis Terrace, look out for Hedd Môr, once the home of Elizabeth Mary Jones (Moelona). She published books for children, school text books and novels.

that Dylan describes in *Quite Early One Morning*, with "the town behind and below" him. It's a walk you can leave for another day.

In the meantime, let's spare a thought for one of Llareggub's most loveable characters: sweet-singing, floor-scrubbing Polly Garter, happy in her garden that grows only washing and babies. She who loves children and loves loving, as Dylan's cast list simply describes her.

> Polly's original went regularly to Towyn chapel and also scrubbed its steps. Like Polly, she was a cleaner and scrubbed the floors of many of the houses in dirt-defying New Quay.

> She's mentioned by name in *Quite Early One Morning*, and in early drafts of *Under Milk Wood*.

> She certainly loved children ("I've got eight," she often boasted) and they loved her back: "She was like a honey pot – the children were always coming home to her. A wonderful mother."

> She was honest and down to earth: "Babies are made at the bottom of the garden" was one of her favourite sayings.

> She was flamboyant and vivacious: "There was something about her that was different, and Dylan would have noticed that and liked it."

> She was very popular about the town: "She was a lovely person, always smiling and laughing, great fun. She was so loveable – and loyal."

> She liked parties and pubs: "She really loved the men…even when she was seventy she was chatting up the young blokes in the pub. She was full of life, she was great. She was *special*."

> She praised the Lord that we are a musical nation: "Oh, she could sing beautifully. She sang in the Hall at concerts, and in Towyn. At parties and

functions, hymns often, duets with her son… people were always asking her to sing."

She was a motherly soul mate, nine years older than Dylan, someone who often…

Yes, but what was her name?

Well, that's New Quay's secret. So relax, enjoy your drink, watch the dolphins dive through the hoop of the setting sun, and wait for the thin night to darken as this little town at the far end of Wales springs awake, and the bad good boys from the faraway farms slip into town.

*Oh, isn't life a terrible thing, thank God?*

# NEW QUAY: LOCAL INFORMATION

*AREA*: 279 acres

*POPULATION*: 1945 Register of Electors: 877; 1931 Census: 1,112

*WELSH SPEAKERS*: 1931 Census: 880

*BANKS*: Barclays, Church Street; Lloyds, Hill Street; Midland, Margaret Street; National and Provincial, Pengeulan.

*EARLY CLOSING DAY*: Wednesday

*FACTORY*: A factory plant for the production of gyroscopic indicators, for use in aerial navigation, was erected by Messers. Reid and Sigrist, under the aegis of the Ministry of Aircraft Production in the autumn of 1945. The factory occupies the site of the old Storehouse in Lower Church Street and is considered to be one of the most up-to-date factories of its kind in Wales.

*HARBOUR CO*: Hon. Treasurer, Mr DE Phillips, Adpar

*MEDICAL OFFICER OF HEALTH*: Dr DRT Griffiths

*MEMORIAL HALL*: Erected 1924-25, accommodates about 800. Hon. Secs: Mr JB Roberts, Ironmonger, and Mr Trevor Harries, Central Pharmacy.

*MOTOR INDEX MARK*: EJ

*ORDNANCE MAPS* are on sale from local booksellers. The New Popular One-Inch Maps, Nos. 139, 127 and 140 (Prices: paper flat, 2s., paper folded, 2s. 3d.) cover New Quay and District.

*POSTAL FACILITIES*: Deliveries 8.40am and 1.55pm

*RAILWAY STATION*: New Quay has no railway station of its own but this comparative remoteness does not seem to deter the discriminating holiday maker.

*RATEABLE VALUE*: £3,743. Sum represented by a penny rate: £15 approx.

*RATES*: General 20/6 per annum. Water 2s per annum.

*RN LIFE-BOAT INSTITUTION*: The New Quay Station was established in 1864. Local Hon. Sec: Mr DB Rees, Park Hill.

*SHOP HOURS*: 9am to 6pm. Hours extended during holiday season.

*URBAN DISTRICT COUNCIL*: Mr Eifion Price (Chairman), Mrs SM Davies (Vice-Chairman), Mr DB Rees, Mr E Arden Davies, Mr Evan Jones, Mr RIP Jones, Mr W. Cherry, Mr Dewi Rees, Mr Donald Evans. Clerk to the Council: Mr J. Amphlett Lewis.

## CHURCHES AND CHAPELS OF THE DISTRICT

*LLANLLWCHAIARN PARISH CHURCH* is a neat, Gothic building consisting of nave, chancel, porch and vestibule, and ornamental tower and spire. Its patron saint is Llwchaiarn, son of Hygarvael ap Cyndrwyn, a prince of Powys, who flourished in the sixth century. The present building, erected in 1865, is on the site of the old structure. Registers commence in 1720 and the Transcripts in 1674. Services: Welsh at 10am and 6pm. English at 11am.

*TABERNACLE (Welsh Presbyterian)*. The first building was erected in 1807. The interior was entirely reconstructed in 1926, and furnished throughout in dark oak. It is one of the most commodious Cardiganshire chapels and its handsome pipe organ dates from 1896. Services: 10am and 6pm.

*TOWYN (Welsh Congregational)*. Built in 1861, this is a commodious building with a modern pipe organ. Services: 10am and 6pm.

*BETHEL (Welsh Baptist)*. Built in 1849. The cause is an offshoot of the one at Llwyndafydd. Services: 10am and 6pm.

# A Tern about the Cliffs:
# New Quay to Llanina and back

**2 miles**

OS Landranger 145 and 146, Explorer 198

There may be many visitors who want to do only the New Quay end of the Trail, so this section describes the route. This is a circular walk, but only if you get your timing right, and start off from New Quay at the beginning of low tide. It's a walk that can be done in reverse by leaving your car at Coed Llanina.

As soon as the receding sea leaves a strip of sand beneath the cliffs, walk down to the Lifeboat Station, and head across the beach towards Llanina Point. After passing the cliffs, look out for a path that goes into the trees, about twenty metres before the large wooden piles that stick out prominently from the sand. There's a pile of large boulders in front of the path to stop erosion.

Take the path up, going right at the first junction, through a beautiful glade of hartstongue ferns. Go past the first house and a white bungalow, around where the path sweeps upwards. Ignore the waymark post and the steps going right, and continue up the slope. Turn left down the side of the green garage. Carry on into the caravan site, following the driveway that goes between caravans on your left and a block of flats on your right. Go straight on at the crossroads and climb up to the main road, where you turn left. Walk along the road, and then a pavement, until you come to the turning for Cei Bach, where you go left. After a few hundred metres, you'll come to Ffynnonfeddyg, a Mediterranean-style villa on your left, whose significance in Dylan's life is described on page 45.

Further along the road, again on your left, is Majoda, where Dylan lived in 1944–45. Detailed information is given on pages 43-46.

Carry on down the hill to Llanina, to the bridge over the river Llethi. It's worth pausing here and taking stock. Upstream, you'll see Coed Llanina, laid out in circular walks, including one that is suitable for wheelchairs. On the other side is a mansion called Plas Llanina and the church of St. Ina, both surrounded by woodland and the sea. Dylan first came here in 1938/39, and his association through the 1940s with Llanina is described on page 41.

Walk through the gates into Plas Llanina. The path to your right goes to the beach but ignore it for the moment. Go straight ahead towards the house, on a public right of way through the wooden gate. Continue

*High Terrace, New Quay, limping visible down to the sea*

up to the house, veering right into the arched entrance-way to the graveyard and church of St. Ina. An outline of the history of the house, church and graveyard is provided on page 42.

Retrace your steps towards the main gates. Just before reaching them, turn left to take the footpath down to Traethgwyn beach. Climb the concrete steps and turn left again for a bracing walk to New Quay. If you've got your timing right, you'll have a fine stretch of sand to walk across. From here on, follow the guidance given in the main text, on pages 48-49.

# Dry Boots, Faint Hearts: the High Tide Routes

## Cei Bach to Llanina

You've descended to a junction with another path, and decided the tide's too high to go down to Cei Bach beach. So walk straight on, following the waymark post. Cross a stile and follow the bottom edge of three fields until you come to Llwynon Farm. Head left across the farmyard to the country road. Turn right and follow the road round to the left. You go downhill a few hundred yards and bear right. This beautiful, winding lane will take you down to Llanina, to the bridge over the river Llethi.

## Ffynnonfeddyg to New Quay

Walk up the road from Ffynnonfeddyg to the junction with the main road, and turn right. Dylan often came this way, first calling for Vera Killick and then waiting at the junction for Thomas Jones the Butcher to join them. You now need to walk a half-mile along the main road, which can be busy in summer. The first part has a pavement, but the second does not, so take great care. Look out for a footpath sign on your right-hand side, opposite a house called Lyndon, which takes you down a drive giving access to Bryn Arian and Traethina. This downhill path to the caravans isn't elevating but it's better than staying on the main road.

At the bottom, go straight across as you enter the caravan site. Walk between a row of caravans on your right, and a two-storey block of flats on your left. It's marked "Private Drive to Traethina" but it is a public right of way. The path goes down the side of the green garage, and then you turn right. A few yards down is a waymark post, where you turn left up some wooden steps. You can now pick up the route again on page 49.

# Trail Extensions: Walks for Another Day

## Eli Jenkins' Pub Walk: Along the Dewi with the Cilie Boys

**7 miles**

OS Landranger 145, Explorer 198

The Dewi flows through Llwyndafydd, a pretty village just a few miles south of New Quay. It rises near Blaencwmpridd Farm, on the other side of the A487 road. It flows past, and is joined by, the waters of the well, Ffynnon Ddewi, where the troops of Henry VII stopped to quench their thirst on their march to Bosworth. The river is sometimes known as the Dewi Fawr, and on OS maps it's usually named as Afon Ffynnon Ddewi.

The walk starts and finishes at the Crown Inn, Llwyndafydd. Park where you can or in the pub car park, though do repay the kindness. This won't be hard to do – it's one of the loveliest pubs in Wales with good food, real ale and a garden and children's play area.

The Crown was much used by the Cilie family of poets. These were the many children and grandchildren of Mary and Jeremiah Jones (1855–1902). They had an extraordinary literary talent and earned their living as farmers, blacksmiths, preachers and sailors. They came to the Crown to read their verses and to sing hymns and folk songs. One of Jeremiah's sons, Simon Bartholomew (1894–1966), won the Crown in the 1933 National Eisteddfod at Wrexham, and the Poet Laureate, John Masefield, travelled there especially to meet him. The *Western Mail* report on the Eisteddfod gave extensive coverage of the Cilie family, as it did when Simon won the Chair in 1936 at Fishguard with *Tyddewi*, his poem about Dewi Sant. Over the years, the paper also published the prose and poems of the Cilie family. They were certainly not poets whose fame was confined to Cardiganshire – the *Western Mail* report on the 1936 Eisteddfod, which Dylan visited, described the Cilie family as a "centre of Welsh culture."

Llwyndafydd is an excellent base for exploring the beautiful Cilie country, and I've listed places to stay in the 'Beds, Beer and Buses' section of the guide. The chapel in the village is worth a visit, too; it's up behind the Crown, next to Neuadd Farm, where Henry VII stayed the night on the way to Bosworth. He must have enjoyed himself, because the next day he got no further than New Quay, where he spent the night in Plas y Wern, Gilfachreda.

We don't know that Dylan came to the Crown, or met his fellow poets, but it's telling that the young Tommy Herbert came here a lot, as did Jack Patrick of the Black Lion, who rode out to the pub on his horse. Tommy Herbert wrote of Dylan in an unpublished essay: "I was surprised at his knowledge of early Welsh poetry, but he had also spent time in the company of contemporary Welsh writers."

The Crown is halfway on a classic pub crawl starting in New Quay and ending in Llangrannog. You can walk from New Quay to Llangrannog and back in a day, picking your way along the coast, or inland along country lanes and footpaths easily found on the Explorer map.

Of course, the Rev. Eli Jenkins would never have gone to a pub, not even to share verses with other poets, or to remind them gravely that his own father died of drink and agriculture. But this is a walk one can imagine that Eli Jenkins might have greatly enjoyed, strolling beside his beloved Dewi to the coast, from whose headland he could see tempestuous Cader Idris, glorious Moel yr Wyddfa and the tell-tales of Pumlumon.

Leave the pub, if you can, and take the turning down to Cwmtydu. The road follows the Dewi all the way to the sea through a wooded, high-sided valley called Cwm Dewi. This whole area is Dewi country – there are two rivers here called the Dewi, a Dewi Sant church, Dewi's Well and several houses and generations of men given the name.

The walk down the valley is at its best in early summer, when the trees are in leaf, and the foxgloves and honeysuckle are out, but it's a wonderful walk at any time of the year. Whatever the season, the Dewi is always full of itself. When puppeteer Walter Wilkinson came this way in the 1940s he heard the Dewi "murmuring, purling, singing, bubbling, gurgling" and gluggity-glugging its way down the valley. The Dewi sings because of the natural stone steps in its bed as it falls to the beach at Cwmtydu.

Eventually you'll come to a small crossroads, with a road going left to Pen y Parc Farm. The river is stronger now because it has been joined by two other rivers – the little Dewi, which rises in the south near a farm called Pwllychwil, and the Bothe. Climb down beside the bridge and look at the natural gully in the river bed. It was through this that the Cilie family and other farmers drove

*Samuel crossing the singing Dewi*

*In a day dream: looking for poets and submarines*

their sheep for dipping, under the close supervision of the local constable. If you followed this road to Pen y Parc for a mile or so, you'd come to Cilie Farm.

Carry on down the road with the smell of the sea getting stronger. From now on, the river is known as the Tudur, derived from Saint Tydu, a Celtic saint from Brittany. The valley opens out into Cwmtydu, with its little shops, beach and natural lagoon – Llyn y Morllyn. There's an old lime kiln here, and romantic intrigue in the air: the cove was much used for smuggling and, locals will tell you, by German submarines looking for fresh water and supplies during the last world war. The Cilie family came here on high days and holidays, not just to sing and recite but for quoits, arm-wrestling, sports and swimming. If the poets were able to swim across the bay and back, they were allowed to carve their names on a rock – Craig yr Enwau – that survived at least to the 1970s but has now been taken away by the sea.

Climb out of the beach up the headland on your right, zig-zagging to the top, ignoring the path that goes straight ahead towards the sea. Once at the top, follow the cliff edge on National Trust land for a mile or so, passing first the Iron Age fort of Castell Bach with its clearly defined banks and ditches. Wilkinson stretched out up here "on a bed of odorous thyme and golden trefoil", and watched seals and porpoises tumbling in the waves – a vast number of them, he wrote, as far as the eye could reach.

Ignore the paths that take you inland. Carry on along the cliff to the next beach, which is mostly shingle with a river running down its middle. Climb out and turn right to walk inland up the valley to Nanternis. The path is clearly marked on the map and on the ground. When you enter woodland for the first time, you'll find a footbridge. Cross it and immediately turn left to walk up the valley – it's signposted "Public Footpath" but on the other side it says "Nanternis". Leave Cwm Soden by a kissing gate. Carry on, ignoring paths going off to your left. You'll eventually come to a stile, gate and road beside a house. Go straight up – don't be tempted by the road to the right that crosses the bridge.

When you reach the road at Nanternis, turn right and go straight on back to Llwyndafydd for a well-earned pint or cup of tea on the banks of the singing Dewi. You'll do a good deal better than Wilkinson did: on his return to New Quay he found an old inn but

*Climbing out of Cwmtydu*

The shelves of the bar, which should have been a galaxy of odd-shaped bottles gleaming with liquid fire, were a melancholy emptiness. There was no food, no tea even, and all I could get hold of was a bottle of stout – that extraordinary black fluid which looks the very opposite of anything one ought to drink.

No chance at all of that happening in the Crown. *Iechyd da!*

# Dylan and Caitlin's Pub Walk: Tal-sarn to Ystrad Aeron

**4 miles**

OS Landranger 146, Explorer 199

Dylan and Caitlin liked to walk from Tal-sarn to the Vale of Aeron pub in Ystrad Aeron (Felin-fach). Dylan was on good terms with the landlord, Thomas Vaughan, who was:

> a good conversationalist and had very good English as well…and he knew current events pretty well…I think he was the attraction for Dylan to come down from Tal-sarn, it's quite a walk, a good three miles. Caitlin and he were down here very often. (Delme Vaughan)

Caitlin may have felt more at ease here than she did in the Red Lion in Tal-sarn:

> The women were all disgusted with Caitlin and Mrs Killick being in the pub. All the women in Tal-sarn had one eye out of the door watching them going in the Red Lion. That's how it was in them days. (Emrys Davies)

Dylan and Caitlin walked along the footpath that went past Llanllŷr Mansion and Glanwern Farm but there's a much better way to get to the Vale of Aeron pub from Tal-sarn.

The walk starts at the Llew Coch (the Red Lion) in Tal-sarn. Walk up to the craft centre in Tŷ Mawr, cross the yard, go through a series of metalled gates and follow the left-hand hedge of the large field to its end until you reach another gate. Turn right onto a track, and then left at the junction. Walk up through the gate past Wern Fach cottage. As you leave the cottage behind, look right across the fields for one of the best views of Gelli Mansion, where Dylan stayed during the war (see page 20).

This wide and overhung track is The Monks' Trod, probably one of the routes used by Cistercian monks to reach their fish traps on the coast. Exit onto a high meadow, and follow the left-hand hedge. There are wonderful views of the Aeron valley below and, to your right, a line of folded hills. Was it here that Dylan was inspired to write, in *A Winter's Tale*, about a farmhouse "cupped in the folds of a vale"?

Carry on along the hedge-line to the far end of the field. Go through the gate and descend the stony track to Brynog Mansion, where you go past the model farm buildings, to turn left at the crossroads in the middle of the farmyard. Walk down the lane, cross the Aeron and up the avenue of rhododendrons to the main road. Turn left. There is no avoiding this stretch of main road but it's only a few minutes walk to the Vale of Aeron. It's still a rather special country pub, much used by villagers, with a quiet, evocative atmosphere.

While you're here, cross the road to the church and look for the grave of John Davies (1722–1799, Shôn Dafydd y Crydd), another Aeron poet. You'll find his grave directly behind the wooden bench by the church door. The inscription reads:

> Beneath this stone lies John alone
> Cordwainer, scribe, Musician,
> Poet sublime in blank and Rhime,
> Devine and Politician.

To return to Tal-sarn, retrace your steps up the main road and go back down the avenue again to Brynog. Just before the bridge over the Aeron, go right over the stile and then stick close to the river all the way to Tal-sarn.

Of course, you can also do the walk in reverse, leaving your car in Ystrad Aeron and having lunch in the Llew Coch.

# Walking with Bonnie: Into the Valley of the Shadow of Debt

In 1930 when he was sixteen, Dylan visited a farm, Yr Hendre, near the border town of St Dogmaels. It's about fifteen miles south of New Quay, as the gull flies (SN 124 473). The large farmhouse and traditional out-buildings are settled in a hollow near the cliffs, with wonderful views southwards to Newport and Fishguard. The farm was run by Lawrence James, who lived there with his mother Margaret and daughter Bonnie.

Lawrence James was a Welsh-speaking, local man whose family had been farmers in and around Eglwyswrw. He took in paying guests for the summer, worked the farm and ran a riding school to boost the family income. Lawrence had been a horse soldier in the First World War in the Pembrokeshire Yeomanry. He is remembered as "a big man, about eighteen stone, very jolly, fit and active, and he loved the horses."

I tracked down Bonnie James to Surrey, where she now lives in retirement from her doctor's practice. She told me that her father was the first in the area to take paying guests. She still has an autograph album with the names of many of Hendre's visitors, some of whom later became prominent in public affairs and the arts. Poet Alun Lewis stayed here in May 1939 with Gweno Ellis, whom he later married. He told a friend that the stay, "was memorable, *mon dieu*, and the sea blue and the water deep around the rocks, and the corn all stooked and warm." [6] The couple came with Ethel James, one of Lawrence's sisters, who was a teacher in Mountain Ash and a close friend of Gweno's. (Lawrence had three sisters, all given priority by their mother Margaret. "My grandmother," recalls Bonnie, "was a feminist. She insisted that women were not just equal to men

---

[6] Quoted in Pikoulis, *Alun Lewis a Life,* 1984. Pikoulis describes the importance of the friendship between Alun Lewis and Richard Mills. In *Oil on Troubled Waters* (1996), I write about Mills' tenure as Deputy Director of the Gulbenkian Foundation from 1960 to 1980. The Director of the Foundation for much of this time was Jim Thornton, once a good friend of Dylan's, and funder of Vernon Watkins' periods of Poet-in-Residence at University College, Swansea.

but were actually superior to them. She ensured that her three girls received an education whereas the boys had to fend for themselves on the farms.")

Other guests included the young Lord Edmund-Davies, drama teacher Rose Bruford, journalist Hannen Swaffer, Col. and Unity Haig (the military not the whiskey branch) and Godfrey Rotter, the renowned explosives expert from the Royal Arsenal at Woolwich, who later moved to the quieter firing ranges of Cilie country, buying a house in the village of Llwyndafydd. Writer R.M. Lockley also came to Hendre, seeking advice from Lawrence James on farming.

Bonnie recalls that Dylan came in the spring of 1930, just after a local eisteddfod that had taken place in Cardigan on March 5, at which she had won first prize for her singing. Dylan came with a cousin of Bonnie's, Cyril James, who seems to have been at school with him in Swansea, and whose father "was in the coal mines". They came by train to Cardigan, and were met by a pony and trap.

Bonnie, who was ten at the time, remembers the young Dylan as "extremely presentable and dishy, not at all the scruffy bohemian, and in sharp contrast to my cousin." Dylan had no knowledge of Welsh, Bonnie told me, "but he was trying to learn it, just little bits here and there… he was vaguely interested… everybody wanted to speak Welsh when they came down to us. It was quite definitely a wish on his part to do so."

Dylan and Cyril spent much of the holiday walking about the coast, with visits in the pony and trap to Cardigan. Dylan wrote a poem for Bonnie, the first entry in her new autograph album, given to her by Ethel James to mark Gŵyl Dewi Sant, St David's Day, on 1 March that year. The poem, also entered into Dylan's notebook on 17 June 1930, is as follows:

To Bonnie

He said, "You seem so lovely, Chloe;
Your pretty body and your hair
Are smoother than the rose and snowy,
Soft as a plum, and light as air.

I give this garland for your head,
This flower for you, and
I give you all I have," he said.
She smiled and took his hand.


The two boys stayed a fortnight. Dylan failed to pay his bill. It took several letters from Ethel James before Dylan's mother eventually settled on his behalf.

There are many walks you can do that take in Yr Hendre, using Outdoor Leisure Map 35. For example, leave your car at the top of the long stone road that descends to the farm, walk down and follow the track to Tre-Rhys, then along into Ceibwr Bay. You can return either by the coast path, or inland via Moylgrove. There are so many paths and quiet lanes here that you can put together your own route, including starting off in Moylgrove. Visit Bethel chapel there, a name that crops up in Dylan's writings through most of his life, and recalls Bethel in New Quay. Bryn Bethel cemetery is just a few fields away from Yr Hendre, as the rabbit runs.

# Trail Diversions:
# Dylan Posers for a Rainy Day

New Quay has a mild and equable climate. Frosts and snow hardly occur. Its fresh air is so beneficial, advised one early guide book, that, "many bent and crippled with sciatica and rheumatism have been known to throw away their sticks and crutches. Pale and delicate youths, leave with ruddy (sun-burnt) cheeks and robust health."

The town, says the guide, "is free from fogs, and zymotic diseases are almost unknown."

And, of course, it doesn't rain very often. But if you are unlucky to be here on one of those rare days when it's raining straight enough to grow runner beans up, then try the following:

## The Majoda Shooting:
## What the Policeman Discovered

In Dylan's day, Majoda was a wood and asbestos shack, looking very much like a 1930s cricket pavilion. There's an artist's impression of the outside on page 43. But what was the inside like? The plan below was commissioned by the police in March 1945 after the shooting incident. As you stand outside Majoda today, perhaps the drawing will give you some idea of what it must have been like for Dylan and his family living here in such cramped conditions through one of the coldest winters on record.

This plan was given to me after the publication of my book, in which I described the shooting at the bungalow and the trial of Captain William Killick, a commando in the SOE. I have also been given the notes made by the arresting officer, PC Islwyn Williams. I reproduce these notes below, together with relevant extracts from the newspaper reports of Killick's trial. I hope these will help you reconstruct the events of the night of 6 March 1945.

# PLAN OF "MAJODA" BUNGALOW,
## CNWC-Y-LILI, NEW QUAY, CARDIGANSHIRE.

PLAN.

*Plan of Majoda*

# The Scene

At about 10.40pm, Dylan was standing in front of the fireplace in the living room at Majoda, telling Caitlin and friends about his scuffle in the Black Lion with William Killick. In Ffynonnfeddyg next door, Killick had also returned from the pub and was retrieving a Sten gun and hand grenade from his store of weapons, intent on giving Dylan and his party a taste of war. Killick walked along the road to Majoda, stood outside the scullery window and fired into the air. This effectively gave warning to the people inside to take cover, which they did. But what happened next?

# The Trial Reports

The *Cambrian News* notes that the police recovered fourteen bullet cases from outside the bungalow; five from within the living room; and three spent bullet heads. It also describes "a short burst through the scullery window." It described the Sten gun as "American-type", and notes that the grenade did not have a detonator. Much of the paper's report on the evidence of Major Kendall of the War Office was left out because of a typesetting error. All that tantalisingly remains is: "the bullet that went through the partition could not have been fired straight; the gun must have been elevated."

*The Welsh Gazette* says there were two bursts of gunfire. The SOE report on the shooting also says that two bursts were fired.

The *News of the World* report contains the following:

> Dylan's evidence: "There was a rattle of machine gun fire and the sound of smashing glass. We all dropped to the floor…There was another burst of firing…bullets came into the house…Then the front door was burst open and Capt. Killick appeared…He then fired a burst into the ceiling of the bungalow."

> Killick's evidence: "At the back of the bungalow I fired a long burst into the air. By a light in the living room I could see that there was no-one in my line of fire. So I fired at a partition, thinking the bullets would not penetrate it. I did not know it was of thin asbestos."

# PC Islwyn Williams' Notes

These notes are not written in the order in which events happened. They seem to be written in the order PC Williams found evidence as he walked from the back of the bungalow to the front. The notes were written on the reverse of the architect's plan.

2[?] holes in glass pane outside scullery window 4-9 above ground level

2 B/Holes in asbestos partition 27in wide[?] one 5/8 [one] 5/11½.

1 graze 6/2½ on L jamb of door leading from kitchen to living room.

In transom of same door 10in from left a bullet hole.

Asbestos partition nr. the rt. of same door bullet hole 4/7¾ by the outside living room kitchen side and 4/9 to the inside.

On the door of bedroom No 2 there was a narrow mark[?] 4/10 high and lodged in the right jamb of the same door was an embedded bullet.

About 29in from wall of bedroom No 2 within ½ an inch of ceiling of the living room facing the sea I found an embedded bullet.

In the ceiling directly in line with the front door I noticed 6 bullet holes in the shape of a horse shoe.

William Killick was an expert marksman. But he had been drinking heavily from lunchtime that day, and he was angry with Dylan and his friends after the scuffle in the Black Lion earlier in the evening. He was not wearing his contact lenses or glasses (which he sometimes wore on active service) so his vision would have been somewhat impaired. There would have been little light spilling over into the darkened kitchen and scullery; not only were there blackout restrictions, but the light in the living room was provided by a calor gas lamp.

A Sten gun has a switch for single shots – the trigger has to be pulled back each time – or for automatic, when the gun keeps on firing ("bursts") as long as the trigger is held back and ammunition is available. It is extremely hard to fire one shot if it is set to automatic; the evidence clearly points to bursts being fired. The Sten gun is notorious for its jerky movements when firing; it is a crude weapon whose effectiveness depends partly on the dispersion or spray of bullets as the gun jerks about in firing. It is particularly prone to jerk upwards. Its unsteadiness is likely to be exacerbated if the person using it is drunk.

So what did happen that night of 6 March? You now have enough information to carry out your own reconstruction, not a bad way to spend a quiet evening in New Quay. And while you're sitting in the pub poring over the plan and notes, you can also put an end to all the embroidered storytelling about the shooting. It's clear that William Killick fired no more than four bullets from outside the scullery window into the bungalow. There is then no basis for accounts that the bungalow was indiscriminately sprayed, raked or riddled with gunfire. Dylan's claim that Killick fired "many rounds" into the bungalow is an exaggeration. There is nothing in PC Williams' notes about bullets passing into Aeronwy's bedroom, or of any being found there.

Did William Killick attempt to murder anyone? The judge didn't think so, and at his trial in June 1945 he directed the jury to acquit on all charges. Dylan had been terrified by the shooting, but his views on the incident were conveyed in a letter of February 1957 from Vernon Watkins to William Killick:

> Of course you did not attempt to murder Dylan, nor even to do
> him bodily injury, and he quite understood this. I can assure you that
> neither in this letter nor in any conversation I had with him did he
> express any malice towards you. He thought you had made a mistake,
> and that was all.

# How Often did Dylan Return to New Quay after 1945?

I hope you'll want to come back to New Quay; there's a lot of good walking in the area, and not just along the coast. There's also the sailing, the beaches, the fishing and the dolphin spotting. There are regattas throughout the summer and an Arts Festival, too. But how often did Dylan himself come back after 1945? He wasn't slow in "lauding" the town, as he put it, and encouraging others to go there – as his letters show.

The question of Dylan's return is intriguing because it has some bearing on the writing of *Under Milk Wood*. Dylan wrote most of the first half in a caravan in South Leigh, Oxfordshire, in 1947/48. The second half was written almost entirely in Boston and New York, in April and May 1953. Fewer than 300 lines, or 17% of the play, were written at the Boat House in Laugharne.

The first half was thus mostly written within three years of Dylan leaving New Quay, presumably with memories still fresh and his Cardiganshire notebooks to hand. If Dylan continued to visit New Quay after 1945, then it would help to explain even further why the town had such an impact on *Milk Wood*. But did he come back?

Dylan himself gives us a few clues; in his radio talk, *The Crumbs of One Man's Year*, broadcast on 27 December 1946, he says he was in New Quay that year. His letter of 29 August 1946 to Margaret Taylor hints strongly at a continuing familiarity with the town. Although Aberaeron-based Thomas Herbert never saw Dylan again after the poet left New Quay in 1945, he kept "getting messages from friends that Dylan had asked to be remembered to me." (unpublished essay).

Confirming these clues, however, is difficult. Dylan led a nomadic life during the 1940s as he sought out work and cheap accommodation. His letters provide many of his addresses but there are large gaps. No lists of electors were kept between 1939 and 1945. If periods of residence are difficult to establish, visits are even harder. In this situation, anyone on the Dylan trail has to rely on 'sightings'.

I mentioned in the text that the author Jon Meirion Jones (1935–) had seen Dylan with Dill Jones in the Commercial in 1946. It was early summer, in the evening, around regatta time, held in early or mid August, depending on the tides. The young Jones was waiting on Commercial Square for the Crosville bus to take him home:

> I lived in Cross Inn for a while (1944–47), and attended Cross Inn C.P. School before moving to Cardigan Grammar School. I spent considerable time in New Quay…I remember listening to Dill Jones, the famous jazz pianist, and friend of Dylan Thomas at the Commercial Hotel. I hasten to add that I was only just coming up to eleven at the time and I only ventured as far as the saloon door, but was fascinated by the genius at the piano. I was informed by another listener regarding the identity, and he also pointed out to me Dylan Thomas, unknown to me at the time. I remember his mop of curly hair and the happy, laughing crew smoking and drinking and listening.

When Jon Meirion Jones wrote to me with this information, I wondered if the incident could have taken place in 1945 when Dylan was at Majoda. I asked Mr Jones if he could be mistaken about the date but he was able to confirm 1946 by reference to other family events.

Dill Jones' naval records show that he was based in Skegness from December 1944. He then sailed for India in June 1945. He returned in January 1946 and was demobbed in June that year. The *Welsh Gazette* of 25 July 1946 noted Jones' return from war duties, and his guest appearance on the radio in Rhythm Club. Dill had probably come to New Quay in the summer of 1946 to join his parents on their annual holiday in the town; Dylan was probably there on his way to, or return from, Ireland.

In my first book, I refer to two reports of Dylan visiting New Quay during the post-war period, one in 1948 in the Dolau pub, then run by Bill and Maudie Bennett who had taken over from Skipper Rymer that year.

Finally, amongst the work sheets of *Under Milk Wood* in the Texas archive is a list from June 1953 of people Dylan intended to write to. It includes Skipper Rymer,[8] who had moved to Berehaven in Eire in the early 1950s. This is another indication that Dylan kept up his New Quay connections.

Telephone 9.

THE

# LION HOTEL

Oldest Established
*FAMILY AND*
*COMMERCIAL*

**Fully Licensed House.**

Beautifully situated close to the sea and convenient for Golf, Tennis and Billiards.

Good Bathing, Boating and Fishing only a few minutes from the Hotel.

**REASONABLE TERMS.**

*Tariff on application to the Proprietresses.*

The Hotel is run under Personal Supervision and every courtesy and attention are assured to guests.

---

[8] The name is 'Rymer' in the 1945 Electoral Register. This is probably the correct spelling but New Quay people have invariably given him an 'h'. Walter Rymer was born in the 1890s. After serving in the army in the 1914–18 war, he became senior captain with Neal and West trawlers in Cardiff. In 1943, he evacuated his family to Sunnydale in New Quay. During the latter part of the war, he became good friends with Dylan, Alastair Graham, Lord Howard de Walden and Ira Jones. Griff Jenkins wrote to me: 'Skipper Rhymer and Ira Jones ran the Dolau (into the ground!). Prior to the Bennetts, Rhymer even re-named it "Fisherman's Rest". Quite often the bar was left unmanned with a notice advising patrons to help themselves, and put the money in the till!'

# The Trail from St Thomas: Dylan's New Quay Relations

Climbing up through the branches of a family tree can be a tedious business, especially if it's not your own. But it's worth the effort in Dylan's case, because it's the best way to get a good view of its adventitious New Quay growth.

Dylan's New Quay family line starts with the children of his maternal grandparents, George and Hannah Williams of 29, Delhi Street, St Thomas, Swansea. George and Hannah were both brought up on farms around Llangain, Carmarthenshire. They moved to Swansea in 1864/66 and George began work on the railways, starting as a porter and moving on to guard, then inspector. They attended Canaan Congregational Church, where George was a deacon and superintendent of the Sunday school; "a very quiet, retiring type of man," said Harry Leyshon, a friend of the family.

George and Hannah had eight children – four boys and four girls. The 1891 census return for 29, Delhi Street, provides the following information, as well as telling us that the whole family spoke both Welsh and English:

| Name | Age | Occupation | Birth Place |
|------|-----|------------|-------------|
| George | 52 | inspector | Carmarthen |
| Hannah | 51 | —— | (illegible)[9] |
| Annie | 28 | dressmaker | Llansteffan |
| John | 26 | railway foreman | Carmarthen |
| Mary Eliz. (Polly) | 25 | music teacher | Swansea |
| David George | 16 | student of medicine | Swansea |
| William Robert | 14 | scholar | Swansea |
| Florence Hannah | 8 | scholar | Swansea |

[9] In the 1871 census, her birthplace is given as Llanstephan.

William Robert (Bob) became a coal trimmer, and David George died at the age of eighteen. Annie later married farmer Jim Jones and lived at Fernhill; Florence married D.J. Thomas, and had two children, Nancy and Dylan. Polly didn't marry; she was a piano teacher and the organist at Canaan. George and Hannah had two other children who were not included in the census return: Thomas, who was first a minister but later "married a woman with money" called Emma Davies. Harry Leyshon has also said that Thomas "had a type of smallholding down West Cross way and he was rather a peculiar character – he was a bit eccentric, I think, something after Dylan's own type...bohemian, in a way." And then there was Dosie who married the Rev. David Rees – classical scholar, botanist, archaeologist and keen member of the Langland Bay Golf Club.

# And so to New Quay...

Dylan's uncle John Williams is something of a mystery. It's said that he owned three houses in St Thomas. He certainly owned 1, Bay View Terrace and 6, Kilvey Terrace – they are noted in his Will. When his wife Elizabeth Ann moved to New Quay, her address on the legal documents was 2, Bay View, but it's not clear whether she or John had bought it.

John was amongst the most prosperous of George and Hannah's children, and was generous in his gifts to other members of the family, including Dylan's parents, Florence and D.J. Thomas, to whom he once gave a piano. Harry Leyshon described John as a "very good friend of Canaan Chapel and I know he presented a Bible and hymnbook for the pulpit."

Paul Ferris has suggested that John had "built up a modest capital, not more than a few thousand pounds, but sufficient in those days to set him apart." John may have owned a small cargo handling company, but there is no trace of it in the Swansea trade directories, though that's not conclusive. We've noted that the 1891 census describes John as a foreman on the railway and still living, aged twenty-six, with his parents in Delhi Street. When he married Elizabeth Ann Evans in 1903, his occupation was given as a foreman coal trimmer – and he was still living at home. Leyshon has confirmed that John "was a foreman on the docks, I think connected with coal shipping and he was really well-off." When John's daughter, Theodosia, was born in 1904, John was described as a stevedore but the address was now 1, Bay View Terrace, a definite step up in the world.

How then did a railway foreman, coal trimmer and stevedore find the money to buy houses and fund his relations? It's unlikely that John married money when he married Elizabeth Ann. The profile of her family in the 1891 census suggests a life of hardship, not prosperity: John Evans, formerly a rollerman, was already dead, and his wife, Elizabeth, aged fifty-eight, lived with their five children at 5, Lamberts Cottages, St Thomas. Elizabeth Ann was a dressmaker; her older brother, William, was a boiler-maker and the younger, Edward, was already working in the Copper Rolling Mills, aged just sixteen. Of her two sisters, Mary Jane was a general servant and Jessie was apprenticed to a dressmaker.

John and Elizabeth Ann were married on 21 December, 1903. She is described as a spinster of thirty-seven years, and he as a bachelor of thirty-nine. Theodosia told Paul Ferris that the marriage had been frowned upon by the Williams family. Perhaps it was, but the marriage certificate seems to provide another side to the story. At the time of the marriage, Elizabeth Ann's address was Paraclete Manse, Newton, the home of Dylan's aunt and uncle, Dosie and David Rees. And it was David Rees who officiated at the wedding in Paraclete Chapel. Moreover, one of the witnesses to the marriage was a certain D.J. Thomas, who just a few days later was married to John's sister, Florence, on 30 December at Castle Street Congregational Chapel, later to become the Kardomah Café where Dylan and his friends hung out.

It seems that John and Elizabeth Ann's marriage had the family seal of approval; the fact that it took place in the village of Newton, Oystermouth, and not in the industrial district of St Thomas, suggests a concern with the niceties of social position. It's possible that Elizabeth Ann brought, not money, but ambition and generosity. She certainly brought elegance, for that's how she's remembered in New Quay today.

When John died, on 4 October 1911, the family were living in 6, Kilvey Terrace, and there were tenants in their house at Bay View. In his will, John left all his estate to Elizabeth Ann. (The Kilvey Terrace house must have been another step up – it had formerly been owned by the manager of the Copper Rolling Mills, with room enough for a live-in servant.)

Theodosia Williams had been born on 5 October 1904, some ten years before her first cousin, Dylan. At the very time that Theodosia was growing up, New

*Evan Joshua James. The inscription reads: 'Presented to Evan James as a token of respect for valuable services by the Lead and Spelter Workers' Union, Swansea, December 1917.'*

Quay's Evan Joshua James was also living in St Thomas. He had moved to Swansea in about 1906, and was an official with the Lead and Spelter Workers' Union at Landore. His children, Nancy and Ieuan, became close friends with Theodosia.

Evan Joshua returned to New Quay in early 1918, and it wasn't long before the widowed Elizabeth Ann and Theodosia were visiting the town to see him and his children. Within a few years, Elizabeth Ann decided to move to New Quay, not least because she hoped that Theodosia's continuing friendship with Ieuan James would blossom into something more. Elizabeth Ann bought a plot of land in 1924 for £69-8s, and Evan Joshua offered to build her a house, Wendawel (sometimes known as Wendowel and Werndawel).

But matters didn't go smoothly, and the friendship between Ieuan and Theodosia broke down. Within a few years, she married Thomas George Legg, the son of a master mariner. George was himself a merchant navy officer whom Theodosia had known in her younger days in St Thomas; he had lived in Bryn Amlwg, Margaret Terrace, and had been taught by Dylan's father at Swansea Grammar School.

The marriage took place in St. Thomas parish church on 15 July 1930. Dylan was sixteen at the time, and it's possible that he went to the ceremony. Theodosia and George Legg came to live in Wendawel after their wedding. There were three children, second cousins to Dylan: Margaret (1930–1998), George (1932–) and Anne (1935–), all brought up in New Quay. Their mother is remembered in the town as "lovely, jolly, beautifully-dressed, always. Lady-like." Another description was "gracious…and never said a bad word about anybody, ever."

*George Williams*

*A note on this photograph makes the following identification: Back row, from the left:
John Williams, Rev. David Rees, Thomas Williams, Bob Williams
Front: Florence, Theodosia and Polly Williams*

*Dylan's aunt, Elizabeth Ann Williams (née Evans) with Theodosia, 1904*

*Elizabeth Ann at Wendawel*

*Dylan's first cousin, Theodosia, in New Quay, 1930s*

*Theodosia's three children: Margaret, George and Anne, 1996*

# Maesgwyn Farm:
# In the Footsteps
# of a Thirsty Poet

*Who milks the cows in Maesgwyn?*

Sometime in the early 1900s, Sarah Evans left the Rhondda for New Quay. It's not clear why she did, but perhaps her husband Evan, who came from Talgarreg, was keen to return to Cardiganshire from the toil of mining coal. For the first few years, Sarah ran the Sailor's Home Arms (later, the Commercial). But she was soon persuaded that it was not right for a Baptist to be serving beer, especially from a pub that was so brazenly close to Bethel chapel. It wasn't long before she moved into Maesgwyn Farm, off Brongwyn Lane. Evan returned from Ferndale to join her, as did two of her children, Hannah Jane and Thomas John, who lived in Tanyfron, just up the slope from Maesgwyn.

'Maesgwyn' literally means 'white or blessed field'. The farm itself stood white against the blue waves of Cardigan Bay. Not only were the farmhouse and stone outbuildings whitewashed, but for most of the year white geraniums grew in pots along the window-sills and in the yard. There was also a large, distinctive white stone marking the entrance to the farm, with a white wall surrounding the front garden, which was usually full of washing and babies – Evan and Sarah had five children, twenty-nine grandchildren (most born or raised in Maesgwyn and Tanyfron) and sixteen great-grandchildren when Sarah died in 1937.

Maesgwyn's fields ran down to the sea. The family kept pigs, cows and a horse called Kruger. There were several apple trees ("leather coats") around the farmhouse, and a very large chestnut tree against which family photographs were often taken.

Sarah moved out after Evans' death in 1932. Thomas John came to live in Maesgwyn with his wife, also Sarah, and took over the farming. Interestingly, Thomas John and his six children were twice related through marriage to

Thomas Davies, who was the tenant farmer at Plas Gelli, Talsarn, at the time that Dylan and Caitlin were living there between 1941 and 1943.

Secluded and leafy Brongwyn Lane was a favourite walk, both for locals and visitors alike. One of Evan and Sarah's great-grandchildren remembers being told about one particular visitor calling for milk:

> ...my great-grandmother sold milk because she had a drawer in a chest – in an old family chest of drawers – that my mother called the Milk Drawer and the milk money used to go in there, and it stood in the hallway of Maesgwyn... my mother said that Dylan Thomas had a mug of milk at Maesgwyn but when that was I don't know as Dylan visited New Quay before 1945.

There was always *Cacen Mamgu Maesgwyn* available in the farmhouse, and no doubt Dylan, with his craving for sweet things, would have had a slice or two with his milk. The buttered cake is still served today by Maesgwyn descendants everywhere.

Thomas John and Sarah were still at Maesgwyn in 1939, as the Register of Electors confirms. A grand-daughter remembers going for tea there in the early years of the war. Thomas John and Sarah moved to Llanarth in 1941 where they both died within a year. It's not clear if anyone moved into Maesgwyn after them. The sea was eating away at the fields and the farm was soon abandoned. It stood empty for many years, a playground for New Quay's children, until one night a high tide brought it crashing to the beach below.

Maesgwyn is still remembered for its grazing cows, apple trees and children. It was truly a place of fecundity, where families and babies flourished, in a milky-white cluster of houses around Brongwyn Lane.

# Cacen Mamgu Maesgwyn

Put the following ingredients into a bowl:

2 mugs of self-raising flower
2 mugs of sultanas
1 mug of dark brown sugar
1 teaspoon of mixed spice
1 egg put into a mug of milk, beaten well and poured onto the mixture
2 tablespoons of melted butter

Mix all the ingredients well. Pour the mixture into a greased and lined 2lb. loaf tin. Bake for one hour at 170 degrees centigrade. Cover with greaseproof paper after twenty minutes to prevent burning. Cool, and serve sliced and buttered.

# Dylan's Wanderings in Cardiganshire

We saw earlier that Dylan's first known visit to Cardiganshire was in 1930, when he visited Cardigan town during his time at Yr Hendre Farm. Dylan may even have come to the county at a much younger age, on holiday with Margaret Phillips and her family – see below. There are also a number of other places in Cardiganshire that have associations with Dylan that you can visit separately, some on foot and others by car.

## Llanarth and Synod Inn

Dylan's experience of Cardiganshire was rooted in his friendship with Vera and Evelyn Phillips, who lived a few streets away in the Swansea Uplands. Their mother, Margaret, had been born in or near Llanarth, just outside New Quay. She was extremely proud of her Cardi roots and frequently visited her relatives in the villages around New Quay. It was Vera, of course, who married William Killick and provided the accommodation at Gelli. Margaret's father came from a farm called Ffôs Helyg, near Synod Inn. The farm was burnt down during the war and nothing remains of it. Its location is SN 402 531 on OS Map 146.

## Lampeter

During the war, Dylan sometimes took a room in the Castle Hotel, usually when he was unable to find peace and quiet at Gelli. He was on good terms with the landlord, Edward Evans, who would sometimes meet up with him in London. Dylan always drank in the Castle's public bar ("he wasn't very fond of the satins and silks"). For much of the time, Dylan was working hard to finish film scripts, according to Evans. Dylan liked walking in the grounds of the College, whose architecture he admired. He enjoyed singing Welsh hymns with the Lampeter rugby team – "He'd love hymns, it was amazing the knowledge he had of Welsh hymns." *Dafydd y Garreg Wen* was his favourite. When travel writer Stuart Mais visited the hotel in 1948, he enjoyed the "Borrovian atmosphere" and Evans' courtesy – "he was preparing a dinner for 40 policemen from Merthyr Tydfil."

In 1953, Dylan was asked to give a reading in Lampeter. He wrote back on 20 June to a Mr Rowland in the town, a brief letter but one with a knock-out punch in the last sentence:

> Thank you for your reply. Yes, certainly, the Friday previous to 19 March 1954 would suit me very well to come along to Lampeter: − I quite understand about your not being able to pay a big fee, but I'm afraid I must ask for five guineas on top of my expenses. Please do let me know if you manage this. And, incidentally, what a long time ahead you do plan! I hope we're not all dead by then.

## Aberystwyth

In 1934, Dylan visited Aberystwyth, where his father had been a student, to see novelist Caradoc Evans:

> Last week-end I spent in Aberystwyth with Caradoc Evans. He's a great fellow. We made a tour of the pubs in the evening, drinking to the eternal damnation of the Almighty & the soon-to-be-hoped-for destruction of the tin Bethels. The university students love Caradoc, & pelt him with stones whenever he goes out.

Dylan came again in 1937 to visit Evans, and saw him intermittently throughout the war years. There were probably other visits to the town, not least because Dylan's friend Kenneth Hancock was a lecturer in the School of Art from 1936. In March 1945, Dylan wrote to Gwyn Jones suggesting a meeting in the town. In 1953, he came to give a poetry reading, and stayed overnight with Jones at his home in Bryn-y-Môr Road, drinking Icelandic schnapps.

The town is mentioned in four of Dylan's works, and it's the hymn *Aberystwyth* that Llareggub's Cherry Owen likes to sing when he's drunk.

## Llangeitho

Dylan liked to walk from Tal-sarn to Llangeitho, and to rest at the Three Horseshoes pub before returning. It's a pretty village in its own right. It was the centre of the Methodist Revival in 1762, led by Daniel Rowland. If you're interested in following the source of the Aeron back to Llyn Eiddwen, Llangeitho is a good place to start from. And while you're at Llyn Eiddwen, look out for the memorial stone to the four Mynydd Bach poets – J.M. Edwards, E. Prosser Rhys, T. Hughes Jones and B.T. Hopkins. Your chances of encountering an American, Patagonian or other exile at the lakeside are surprisingly high; this area was the source of a major exodus. Most families went to Ohio, though some went no further than the coal mines of the Rhondda.

## Talgarreg

Dylan and Caitlin lived in this little village, some five miles inland from New Quay, in 1942. They weren't there very long, and it was probably an escape from Gelli, which could at times get very overcrowded. Bardic poet Dewi Emrys lived in Talgarreg at the time, and Dylan had known him from their London days in the 1930s. Talgarreg is only a couple of miles from Bwlch y Fadfa and Llwynrhydowen, where Dylan's great-uncle, Gwilym Marles, had his chapels. The one at Llwynrhydowen is well worth a visit, though it is falling into disrepair.

The poet Thomas Jacob Thomas (Sarnicol, 1873–1945) was born some two miles down the road to Capel Cynon, in a house called Sarnicol (now a ruin) at SN 398 495. There's a slate plaque in the stone gatepost of the nearby farm, Allt Maen. Sarnicol won the Chair at the National Eisteddfod in 1913 and published ten volumes of verse and prose between 1898 and 1944. Today, the prize-winning poets Donald Evans and Gillian Clarke live in Talgarreg. The pub, the Glanyrafon Arms, is warm and welcoming, and the owners a source of information on local history.

## Llangrannog

Dylan used to visit the Ship Inn at Llangrannog with Tommy Herbert. Perhaps part of the attraction was Dafydd Jones (Isfoel) who wrote witty, and sometimes bawdy, poetry. Isfoel was one of the Cilie family of poets. Tom Jones of the Cilie family kept the Pentre Arms; Dylan visited the pub in 1942/43 with First World War fighter ace, Ira Jones. They helped themselves to beer, but Tom Jones caught them at it and told them to leave. "I say, old boy," protested the

Wing-Commander. "Don't you know who I am?" They were promptly ejected onto the sandy street (Jon Meirion Jones).

The feminist writer Sarah Jane Rees (Cranogwen, 1839–1916) was born and buried here. The stretch of coast between Llangrannog and Tre-saith was the scene for many of the best-selling novels of Allen Raine (Anne Adaliza Evans, 1836–1908). She is buried at the top of Penbryn churchyard. There is also a wonderful beach and woods at Penbryn, run by the National Trust.

The poet Alun Lewis spent most of his boyhood holidays in Penbryn from 1925 onwards. He and his wife Gweno also spent time in Llangrannog and Cwmtydu. Lewis' feelings for the stretch of Cardiganshire coast between Penbryn and New Quay are beautifully caught in his 1942 poem *On Embarkation*.

Edward Elgar had been another visitor to Llangrannog, travelling here in 1901 by train and ox-cart. It's still an unspoilt village on the edge of a sandy cove, and its cliffs provide one of the best places from which to see dolphins.

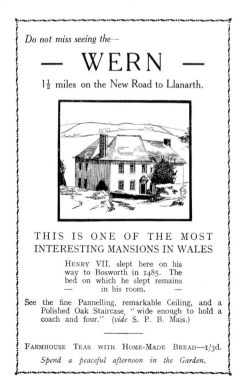

*Do not miss seeing the—*

— WERN —

1½ miles on the New Road to Llanarth.

THIS IS ONE OF THE MOST INTERESTING MANSIONS IN WALES

HENRY VII. slept here on his way to Bosworth in 1485. The bed on which he slept remains — in his room. —

See the fine Pannelling, remarkable Ceiling, and a Polished Oak Staircase, "wide enough to hold a coach and four." (*vide* S. P. B. Mais.)

FARMHOUSE TEAS WITH HOME-MADE BREAD—1/3d.

*Spend a peaceful afternoon in the Garden.*

# Gilfachreda

This is a small village, a few miles outside New Quay. Dylan came here to visit Alastair Graham, who lived in Plas y Wern. This distinctive and attractive house can be seen from the main road; there's also a footpath that skirts close by the curiously-named river, the Euphrates, that runs through the grounds. Henry Tudor is reputed to have slept at Plas y Wern on his way to the Battle of Bosworth. The more exotic visitors during Dylan's time are described on page 72.

Other Cardiganshire places that we know Dylan visited include Cross Inn (New Quay), New Inn and Cardigan again in 1944 – "filthy town" – where he went to a farmers' fair, and met Vernon Watkins' sister, Dot. He wrote a bawdy poem featuring the pub at Cross Inn: *Sooner than you can water milk…* is in *Dylan Thomas: The Poems* edited by Daniel Jones, 1991. Dylan also visited the border towns of Machynlleth and Newcastle Emlyn.

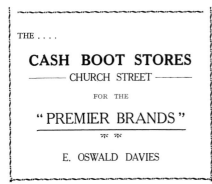

# Dylan's Life: A Brief Chronology

1914    Born in Swansea, October 27th

1934    *18 Poems* published

1936    *Twenty-five Poems* published

1937    Marries Caitlin Macnamara

1938    Moves to Laugharne for six months

1938/39 First visit to Plas Llanina, New Quay

1939    Llewelyn is born; Dylan moves back to Laugharne for nine months; *The Map of Love* is published

1940    *Portrait of the Artist as a Young Dog* is published

1941    Another brief stay in Laugharne; does not return to live there until 1949

1941/43 Stays in Gelli, Tal-sarn, with visits to New Quay

1943    Aeron is born

1944    Moves to New Quay in September; writes *Quite Early One Morning* and starts to write *Under Milk Wood*

1945    Shooting incident at Majoda in March; leaves New Quay in July and moves to Magdalen College, Oxford, in December

1946    *Deaths and Entrances* published; writes five of the precursors to *UMW*

1947    Writes *Return Journey*, one of the most important precursors to *UMW*; moves to South Leigh, Oxfordshire; writes most of first half of *UMW* in 1947/48

1949    Visits Prague and reads extracts from *UMW*; moves to the Boat House, Laugharne, in May; Colm is born

1950    First American trip

1952    Second American trip; *Collected Poems* published; his father dies

1953    Third and fourth American trips; he writes the second half of *UMW* in America; first performance of the play in New York in May; first full British reading in Porthcawl in August. Dylan dies on 9 November, St. Vincent's Hospital, New York

1954    First British performance of *UMW*, BBC Third Programme, January 25th

# Beds, Beer and Buses

Most of the following is taken from the Ceredigion Tourist Information brochure.

★ = the rating provided by the Wales Tourist Board, though not all establishments choose to apply for grading.

## Llanon

The Barn House ★★ 01974 202581
Frondolau Farm Guest House ★★ 01974 202354
Plas Morfa Hotel and Restaurant ★★ 01974 202415
Central Hotel 01974 202969

## Tal-sarn

Abermeurig Mansion ★★★★ 01570 470216
Brynog Mansion ★★★ 01570 470266

The following are not within walking distance of Tal-sarn, but they may agree to collect and return you by prior arrangement:

Dremddu Fawr Farm ★★★ 01570 470394 (a winner of the All Wales Top Cook competition)
Gwarffynnon Farm ★★★ 01570 423583
Taxis are also available to take you from Tal-sarn to Lampeter, where there is plenty of accommodation. See the list of taxi services at the end of this section.

## Ciliau Aeron

Tyglyn Aeron Hotel 01570 470625
Tyglyn Holiday Estate ★★★ 01570 470684 (self-catering bungalows)
Tŷ Lôn Guest House ★★★ 01570 470726

## Aberaeron

Coedmor ★★★ 01545 571615

Hazeldene Guest House ★★★★ 01545 570652

Llys Aeron Guest House ★★★★ 01545 570276

Monachty Arms Hotel ★★ 01545 570389

Arosfa Guest House ★★★ 01545 570120

Lima House ★★★ 01545 570720

The Feathers Royal Hotel 01545 571750

Harbourmaster Hotel (awaiting grading) 01545 570755


## Lampeter

Haulfan ★★★ 01570 422718

Castle Hotel 01570 422554 (where Dylan sometimes stayed)

Black Lion Hotel 01570 422172

The Falcondale Hotel 01570 422910


## New Quay

Arfon View ★★★ 01545 560837 (once the home of Griff Jenkins, a good friend of Dylan and of Augustus John, who both came to eat here)

Myrtle Hill ★★★ 01545 560399

Ffynnonfeddyg ★★★★★ 01545 560222 (where William and Vera Killick lived)

Brynarfor Hotel ★★ 01545 560358

Black Lion Hotel 01545 560209

Hotel Penwig 01545 560910

Cambrian Hotel ★★ 01545 560295

Tŷ Cerrig Guest House ★★★★ 01545 560850

The Hungry Trout 01545 560680


## Cilie Country

Self-catering:

Neuadd Farm Cottages, Llwyndafydd ★★★★★ 01545 560324 (where Henry VII stayed the night)

Glan y Don, Cwmtydu ★★★★ 029 2075 6899

Springfield Cottage, Penbontrhydyfothau ★★★ 01527 892913

Nanternis Farm, Nanternis ★★★★ 01545 560181
Bed and Breakfast:
Llainfran House, Nanternis (awaiting grading) 01545 561243
Berry Green, Blaencelyn ★★★ 01239 654678

## Country Pubs on the Trail

The Ship, Pennant 01545 570355
The Poacher's Pocket, Cilcennin 01570 470320 (formerly the Commercial Inn)
The Vale of Aeron, Ystrad Aeron (Felin-fach) 01570 470385
The Crown, Llwyndafydd 01545 560396
Llew Coch, Tal-sarn 01570 471215

## Taxi Services

Aberaeron and New Quay:
TAR Taxis 01545 560688
Tidy Taxis 01545 561100
Llanon:
Central Taxis 01974 202969
Lampeter:
Ron's Taxis 079 70100233
3 'J's' Taxis 077 73905955

## Tourist Offices

Aberaeron 01545 570602 and aberaeronTIC@ceredigion.gov.uk
New Quay 01545 560865 and newquayTIC@ceredigion.gov.uk (This office is
only open during the season)

They will provide up-to-date information on accommodation and other
matters, as well as a free leaflet on bus and train services in the county. You can
also get bus information on 0870 6082608. Stagecoach and Arriva run an express
coach service that stops in Aberaeron and Llanon – it starts in Cardiff and calls in
other south Wales towns on its way to north Wales. The nearest train station is
Aberystwyth, with a bus and taxi service to Llanon from outside the station. You
can also take a train to Carmarthen, and then a bus to Aberaeron.

# Acknowledgements

The walking and the writing have been enjoyable tasks. Many thanks for the help, and sometimes the company, of Stevie Krayer, Keith and Jacqui Davies, Phyllis Cosmo-Jones, Peter Chetcuti, Eunice Thomas, Samantha Wynne Rhydderch, Michael Williams, Griff Jenkins, Jacqui Lyne, Roger Seal, Ieuan Williams, Eleanor Lister, Margaret Evans, Sue Passmore, Jean and Joe Bugeja, Paul Boland, David Birch and the late Delme Vaughan.

Most of the information on Evan Joshua James and on Theodosia Legg's family came from: Phyllis Cosmo-Jones, whose aunt Maggie Beatrice was married to Evan Joshua; Nell Highet, Evan Joshua's grand-daughter; George Legg, Dylan's second cousin; and Skyrme and Elaine May. Further details came from the Registrar of Births and Marriages in Swansea, the 1891 Census and Kelly's Directories of South Wales. Paul Ferris was, as always, an enthusiastic source of information – I am grateful for having the benefit of the notes of his interview with Theodosia Legg.

Information on Dill Jones came from his sister Barbara Cassini, Wyn Lodwick, George Joslyn, David Griffiths, Griff Jenkins, Alun Morgan and Emma Kendon of Trinity College of Music, London.

Many thanks to John and Wendy Williams for a copy of PC Islwyn Williams' notes of the Majoda shooting, and the architect's plan of the bungalow. Peter Davies helped me re-construct the shooting incident, and extended my knowledge of the uses and abuses of the Sten gun.

Information on the master mariners of New Quay was provided by Griff Jenkins, Keith Davies, Sue Passmore and Kelly's Trade Directories.

My thanks to Bonnie Luscombe, Stanley Davies and John Rees Phillips, who generously provided the information on Yr Hendre.

I am grateful to those who helped me understand more about the Cilie and Aeron poets, including Jon Meirion Jones, John Emrys Jones, Kenneth Jones, Tommy Jones, Eric Jones, Stephen and Megan Morgan, Delyth Thomas, Ralph Richards and Joyce Jenkins.

The Dylan Thomas Trail has become a reality through the commitment and work of Wendy Campion, Public Rights of Way Officer at Ceredigion County

Council. Some of the footpaths on the Trail were renovated with the help of European funding.

As ever, the staff of the National Library of Wales made the research easy and pleasurable, as did Helen Palmer at the Ceredigion Archive. Thanks to the Dylan Thomas Estate and David Higham Associates for permission to quote from Dylan's poems and letters: *Under Milk Wood, Collected Letters, Collected Poems* and *Quite Early One Morning*, all published by Dent, and from the Dylan Thomas archive in the University of Texas at Austin. In the section on New Quay, quotations from *Under Milk Wood* are in italics. Unless otherwise attributed, all other quotations in this section are from *Quite Early One Morning*. A draft of the letter on page 122 to Mr Rowland is amongst the worksheets for the play in Texas, and is not in *Collected Letters*. The quotations from Harry Leyshon are from the Colin Edwards archive in the National Library of Wales. I am grateful to Gwen Watkins for permission to quote from Vernon Watkins' letter to William Killick, and to Rebekah Gilbertson for showing it to me.

*Photographs and illustrations*: I am very grateful to Ken Day for the hard work and inspiration that went into his landscape and seascape photographs.

For the period photographs, my thanks to John and Wendy Williams, Jennifer Davies, Keith Davies, George and Jean Legg, Stephen Morgan, Margaret Evans, Kenneth Jones, Nell Highet, Barbara Lenz, Betty Davis, Stan and Eleri Thomas, Ralph and Kathleen Richards; and Jacky Piqué for the sketch of Majoda. I am indebted to William Howells and the Ceredigion Public Library, Aberystwyth, for permission to reproduce photographs from their collection. Thanks to Gwasg Gomer for permission to reproduce the photograph in *Llambed Ddoe* of Dan Jenkins, and the copyright of the photograph's owner is acknowledged. The photographs of George Williams and of his children came from the National Library of Wales.

The manufacture of a book is a team effort: my thanks to Stevie Krayer for proof-reading and much, much else, and to Lefi and Ceri at Y Lolfa.

I have made use of the following publications, which provide a source of further reading:

# Cardiganshire

*Aberaeron and Mid Ceredigion: Old Photographs* (1994)
  Dyfed Cultural Services Dept.

L. Allan, *Walking the Cardigan Bay Coast* (2000), Kittiwake

*Canmlwyddiant Capel Hermon, Trichrug 1882–1982*, Capel Hermon

G.E. Evans, *Cardiganshire: A Personal Survey* (1903), *Welsh Gazette*

M.L. Evans, *Llanerchaeron: A Tale of Ten Generations 1634–1989* (1996)

D. Jenkins, *Cardiff Tramps, Cardi Crews: Cardiganshire Shipowners and Seamen in Cardiff c.1870-1950* ,*Ceredigion*, Vol X, No. 4 (1987)

B.A. Jones, *Y Byd o Ben Trichrug* (1959), Cymdeithas Lyfrau Ceredigion

S. Rees, *A Guide to Ancient and Historic Wales: Dyfed* (1992), HMSO

D.J. Saer, *The Story of Cardiganshire* (c.1912), Educational Publishing Company

J.H. Salter, *The Flowering Plants and Ferns of Cardiganshire* (1935), Cardiff University Press

G.I. Thomas, *Captain John Richards (1813–1903) and the 'Eagle Eyed' (1858–1897), Ceredigion*, Vol X, No. 4 (1987)

# History of and Guides to New Quay

*A Guide to New Quay. Being a Short Description of New Quay as a Watering Place*, (1895), The Welsh Press

S. Campbell-Passmore, *Farmers and Figureheads: the Port of New Quay and its Hinterland* (1992), Dyfed C.C.

E.B. Davies, *The Story of New Quay* (1933), Llysawel Bookshop, New Quay

G. Davies, *New Quay: The Official Guide* (c.1936), New Quay U.D.C.

M. Evans, *Atgofion Ceinewydd* (1961), Cymdeithas Lyfrau Ceredigion

E. Joshua James, *A Street of Memories, Welsh Gazette* (1959), July 30th

W.J. Lewis, *New Quay and Llanarth* (1988)

D. N. Thomas, *Dylan's New Quay: More Bombay Potato than Boiled Cabbage, New Welsh Review* (2002), 55

*New Quay: The Official Guide* (1948), New Quay U.D.C.

*The New Quay Chronicle*, August 1902

## Other Guides and Travel Books

W. Watkin Davies, *A Wayfarer in Wales* (1930), Methuen

*Gossiping Guide to Wales* (1954), Hughes

E.R. Horsfall-Turner, *Walks and Wanderings in Cardiganshire* (c.1902), Horsfall-Turner

E. Lewes, *A Guide to Aberayron and the Aeron Valley* (1920)

S.P.B. Mais, *I Return to Wales* (1949), Johnson

H.V. Morton, *In Search of Wales* (1947), Methuen

W.T. Palmer, *Wales: It's History and Romance, Where to Go and What to See* (1932), Harrap

*The Rough Guide to Wales* (1998), The Rough Guides

R.W. Thompson, *An Englishman Looks at Wales* (1937), Arrowsmith

W. Wilkinson, *Puppets in Wales* (1948), Bles

## Other Source Material

Paul Ferris, *Dylan Thomas: The Biography* (1999), Dent

J. Pikoulis, *Alun Lewis: A Life* (1984), Poetry Wales Press

D.M. Thomas, *Under Milk Wood: the Definitive Edition* (1995), eds. W. Davies and R. Maud, Dent

D.N. Thomas, *Oil on Troubled Waters: the Gulbenkian Foundation and Social Welfare* (1996), Directory of Social Change

*Dylan Thomas: A Farm, Two Mansions and a Bungalow* (2000), Seren

*Under Milk Wood's birth-in-exile*, in *New Welsh Review* (2001), Spring

## The Aeron Poets

Dinah Davies, *Llinellau Gwasgaredig* (1912), James

D.E. Davies, *Cewri'r Ffydd* (1999), Gomer

J.E. Davies, *James Hughes: Cyfrol Goffa* (1911), Gee

D. Davis, *Telyn Dewi* (1824), Longman

D.I. Edwards, ed. *Cerddi Cerngoch* (1994), Pwyllgor Coffa Cerngoch

D. Jenkins, ed. *Cerddi Cerngoch* (1904), Cwmni y Wasg Eglwysig Gymreig

*Cerddi Ysgol Llanycrwys* (1934), Gomer

J. Jenkin, ed. *Gemau Ceredigion: A Collection of Welsh Poems written by Cardiganshire Poets* (c. 1914), 3 vols. The Educational Publishing Company

J. Jenkins, *Diary of a Welsh Swagman, 1869–1894* (1975), Macmillan

G.M. Roberts: *Y Ddinas Gadarn: Hanes Eglwys Jewin Llundain* (1974)

## The Cilie Poets

J. Meirion Jones, *Teulu'r Cilie* (1999), Cyhoeddiadau Barddas

## Dill Jones

Surprisingly, there is no biography of Dill Jones. Most jazz reference books have a brief entry for him, but the following also provide further material. Griffiths is the most helpful with an outline musical biography and a comprehensive discography. It's in the National Library of Wales but you can also order a copy from Gerard Bielderman, Leie 18, 8032 ZG, Zwolle, Netherlands (00 31 (0)38 4537821).

*Dill Jones* in *Jazz Journal*, November 1952

*Meet Dill Jones* in *Melody Maker* 1953 (month not known)

M. Basini, *Dancing Fingers* (1984), in the *Western Mail*, August 10

D. Griffiths, *Dill Jones: A Discography* (1996), Bielderman

J.H. Klee, *Dill Jones' Gutter Music* in *The Mississippi Rag* (1979), vi/4,7

A. Morgan, *Jones the Jazz* in *Jazz Journal* (2002), March

S.A. Worsfold, *Dill Jones —That Hwyl Feeling* in *Jazz Journal* (1983), March

*Dill Jones Talks to Peter Clayton*, BBC radio broadcast, August 6, 1972

*Ar y Brig: A Profile of Dill Jones*, BBC Wales Television,

    1979 (month not known)

*I Remember Dill*, BBC Radio Wales, *Jazz Juice*, June 27 1994

D. N. Thomas, *Striding Dill Jones: Jazz with Black Hwyl*, *Planet,* June (2002)

Dillwyn Owen Jones (1923–1984) became an internationally famous jazz pianist. His father, John Islwyn Jones, was from New Quay and his mother Lavinia from Cardiff. Jones' paternal grandparents were also New Quay people: his grandfather was D.O. Jones, who became a photographer after serving some years as a Methodist minister. His studio was in Park Street, and he published a series of *Views of New Quay*. Dill Jones was born in Newcastle Emlyn but brought up in Talgarth and Llandovery, where his father was the manager of

Lloyds Bank. The young Jones spent most weekends and holidays in New Quay, where he attended Tabernacle, the chapel in which his aunt, Isawel Jones, played the organ.

After leaving Llandovery College, Jones worked in a bank, before joining the Royal Navy in 1942, and was stationed in Britain until sailing for India in June 1945. He returned to the UK in January 1946, and was demobbed in June. He worked in Lloyds Bank, Westminster, before enrolling to study piano and organ at Trinity College of Music (1946–48). He began his jazz career with Carlo Krahmer and Humphrey Lyttelton (1947–48), and performed at the first Nice Jazz Festival in 1948. Jones recorded with the BBC Jazz Club Band in 1949, introducing the programme on radio and television throughout the 1950s. He settled in New York in 1961 and became associated with several traditional and mainstream players.

Dill Jones' career was cut short by cancer of the throat. He was made a member of the Gorsedd after his death on June 22 1984.

*Dill Jones, c.1954, London Gliding Club, Dunstable*

**Wales within your reach: an attractive series at attractive prices!**

**1. Welsh Talk**
Heini Gruffudd
086243 447 5
£2.95

**6. Welsh Railways**
Jim Green
086243 551 X
£3.95

**2. Welsh Dishes**
Rhian Williams
086243 492 0
£2.95

**7. Welsh Place Names**
Brian Davies
086243 514 5
£3.95

**3. Welsh Songs**
Lefi Gruffudd (ed.)
086243 525 0
£3.95

**8. Welsh Castles**
Geraint Roberts
086243 550 1
£3.95

**4. Welsh Mountain Walks**
Dafydd Andrews
086243 547 1
£3.95

**9. Welsh Rugby Heroes**
Androw Bennett
086243 552 8
£3.95

**5. Welsh Organic Recipes**
Dave and Barbara Frost
086243 574 9
£3.95

**10. Welsh National Heroes**
Alun Roberts
086243 610 9
£4.95

**www.ylolfa.com**
Y Lolfa Cyf., Talybont, Ceredigion SY24 5AP
*e-mail* ylolfa@ylolfa.com